BASIC TEXTS IN COUNSELLING AND PSYCHOTHERAPY

Series editor: Stephen Frosh

This series introduces readers to the theory and practice of counselling and psychotherapy across a wide range of topic areas. The books appeal to anyone wishing to use counselling and psychotherapeutic skills and are particularly relevant to workers in health, education, social work and related settings. The books are unusual in being rooted in psychodynamic and systemic ideas, yet being written at an accessible, readable and introductory level. Each text offers theoretical background and guidance for practice, with creative use of clinical examples.

Published

Jenny Altschuler
WORKING WITH CHRONIC ILLNESS

Bill Barnes, Sheila Ernst and Keith Hyde
AN INTRODUCTION TO GROUPWORK

Stephen Briggs
WORKING WITH ADOLESCENTS

Alex Coren
SHORT-TERM PSYCHOTHERAPY

Emilia Dowling and Gill Gorell Barnes
WORKING WITH CHILDREN AND PARENTS THROUGH SEPARATION AND DIVORCE

Loretta Franklin
AN INTRODUCTION TO WORKPLACE COUNSELLING

Gill Gorell Barnes
FAMILY THERAPY IN CHANGING TIMES 2nd Edition

Sally Modyes
COUNSELLING ADULTS WITH LEARNING DISABLITIES

Ravi Rana
COUNSELLING STUDENTS

Tricia Scott
INTEGRATIVE PSYCHOTHERAPY IN HEALTHCARE

Geraldine Shipton
WORKING WITH EATING DISORDERS

Laurence Spurling
AN INTRODUCTION TO PSYCHODYNAMIC COUNSELLING

Paul Terry
WORKING WITH THE ELDERLY AND THEIR CARERS

Jan Wiener and Mannie Sher
COUNSELLING AND PSYCHOTHERAPY IN PRIMARY HEALTH CARE

Shula Wilson
COUNSELLING ADULTS WITH LEARNING DISABILITIES

Invitation to authors

The Series Editor welcomes proposals for new books within the Basic Texts in Counselling and Psychotherapy series. These should be sent to Stephen Frosh at the School of Psychology, Birkbeck College, Malet Street, London, WC1E 7HX (e-mail s.frosh@bbk.ac.uk)

**Basic Texts in Counselling and Psychotherapy
Series Standing Order ISBN 0–333–69330–2**
(outside North America only)

You can receive future titles in this series as they are published by placing a standing order. Please contact your bookseller or, in the case of difficulty, write to us at the address below with your name and address, the title of the series and the ISBN quoted above.

Customer Services Department, Macmillan Distribution Ltd
Houndmills, Basingstoke, Hampshire RG21 6XS, England

Invitation to authors

The Series Editor welcomes proposals for new books within the Basic Texts in Counselling and Psychotherapy series. These should be sent to Stephen Frosh at the School of Psychology, Birkbeck College, Malet Street, London, WC1E 7HX (email s.frosh@bbk.ac.uk).

Basic Texts in Counselling and Psychotherapy
Series Standing Order ISBN 0-333-69330-2
(outside North America only)

You can receive future titles in this series as they are published by placing a standing order. Please contact your bookseller or, in the case of difficulty, write to us at the address below with your name and address, the title of the series and the ISBN quoted above.

Customer Services Department, Macmillan Distribution Ltd,
Houndmills, Basingstoke, Hampshire RG21 6XS, England

AN INTRODUCTION TO SYSTEMIC THERAPY WITH INDIVIDUALS

A Social Constructionist Approach

FRAN HEDGES

palgrave
macmillan

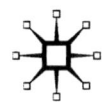

©Fran Hedges 2005

All rights reserved. No reproduction, copy or transmission of this publication may be made without written permission.

No paragraph of this publication may be reproduced, copied or transmitted save with written permission or in accordance with the provisions of the Copyright, Designs and Patents Act 1988, or under the terms of any licence permitting limited copying issued by the Copyright Licensing Agency, 90 Tottenham Court Road, London W1T 4LP.

Any person who does any unauthorised act in relation to this publication may be liable to criminal prosecution and civil claims for damages.

The author has asserted her right to be identified as the author of this work in accordance with the Copyright, Designs and Patents Act 1988.

First published 2005 by
PALGRAVE MACMILLAN
Houndmills, Basingstoke, Hampshire RG21 6XS and
175 Fifth Avenue, New York, N.Y. 10010
Companies and representatives throughout the world

PALGRAVE MACMILLAN is the global academic imprint of the Palgrave Macmillan division of St. Martin's Press, LLC and of Palgrave Macmillan Ltd. Macmillan® is a registered trademark in the United States, United Kingdom and other countries. Palgrave is a registered trademark in the European Union and other countries.

ISBN-13: 978 1403904508   paperback
ISBN-10: 14039 04502   paperback

This book is printed on paper suitable for recycling and made from fully managed and sustained forest sources. Logging, pulping and manufacturing processes are expected to conform to the environmental regulations of the country of origin.

A catalogue record for this book is available from the British Library.

A catalog record for this book is available from the Library of Congress.
Library of Congress Catalog Card Number: 2004061674.

10 9 8 7 6 5 4 3
14 13 12 11 10 09 08 07

Printed in Great Britain by Biddles Ltd, King's Lynn, Norfolk

Dedicated to the memory of Gianfranco Cecchin

Contents

List of figures viii

Acknowledgements ix

1 Introduction 1

2 Overview of Systemic Therapy: Theory/Practice 8

3 Social Constructionist Approaches to Emotion and the Self 27

4 The Importance of Context 47

5 From Neutrality and Curiosity to Self–Other-Reflexivity 66

6 Circular Questioning 83

7 Hypothesising and Systemic Story Creation 100

8 Future Dreaming and Appreciating Abilities 119

9 Tracking an Episode 138

10 Change: an Ethical Stance 156

Appendix 1 The Milan Method: The Five-Part Session 176

Appendix 2 Proforma: Introductory Consultation devised for the Counselling Service: Roehampton University 178

Glossary 180

Bibliography 185

Index 193

LIST OF FIGURES

1	Pearce's 'atomic' model	52
2	Genogram of Angela's family	85
3	Mindmap: making connections when hypothesising	104

ACKNOWLEDGEMENTS

I am immensely grateful to Peter Lang for introducing me to systemic ideas, for his continued inspiration and for his generous help with this book. I would like to thank members of my team at Roehampton University who supported me whilst I wrote the book, in particular Frances Shaw who read drafts and offered wise suggestions. And I am deeply indebted to the many people with whom I had the privilege of being in conversation: clients, colleagues, supervisees and friends, without whom this book would not have been possible.

1
INTRODUCTION

Now is the time for social constructionism to link with practice
McNamee (2003)

When we meet with an individual we are meeting their networks
Lang (2004)

The present is a moment of great innovation and creativity
Pearce (1995)

For practitioners who use systemic constructionist ideas with individuals, the present is certainly a time of great innovation and creativity. These ideas challenge many long-held ideas about the position of the individual and require both rigour and imagination (Bateson 1981). Those who seek certainty may feel uncomfortable with approaches that invite them to develop new languages and practices. But the remarkable effect on our clients justifies the struggle.

After less than six months of systemic practice, Andrea, a Greek therapist who had many years' experience of using traditional therapeutic approaches, was astonished when her clients started changing for the better after only two or three conversations.

Often just one conversation can help a person tell a very different story and subsequently develop more helpful relationships. Even clients with complex difficulties regularly tell us that these conversations help them to live more hopeful lives without needing frequent therapeutic conversations. Systemic therapists normally negotiate the frequency of meetings with clients, not assuming that we will meet every week: although we may work with a client less frequently we may meet over many months or even years. This gives systemic therapy the description 'brief-long' therapy.

At the same time, unlike practitioners who experience 'heart sink', 'burn out' and the kind of 'depression' that can come from working with intractably sad stories, systemic therapists become energised when we observe the positive effects on the people who come to talk to us. This further encourages us to approach clients with fascination, 'awe and amazement' (Lang and McAdam 1995). And these ways of thinking, talking, acting and feeling can have a positive impact on therapists' own stories and lives.

Andrea was also surprised and delighted to notice that conversations in supervision had 'liberated' her from the fear of always 'getting it wrong' and had loosened some of her 'rigid' self-stories.

Although at first it may appear inconsistent with systemic therapy to work with individuals, as early as 1983 John Weakland, one of Gregory Bateson's research team, wrote about doing 'family therapy with individuals'. And Boscolo and Bertrando (1996) say that whilst developing systemic family therapy two days a week with the Milan Associates, they introduced systemic ideas into their individual work.

My aim in this book is to help practitioners develop the skills, abilities and understanding of systemic constructionist practices well enough to put them into practice. 'Understanding' a word or a concept, Wittgenstein (1953) says, means being able to *use it in a context*: we are only able to put something into practice when we really do understand it (nos 146–55).

This book is indebted to the systemic orientation that originated in the early 1970s in Milan with the Milan team (Hoffman 1981; Selvini et al. 1978, 1980) which was developed by Boscolo and Cecchin (known as the 'post-Milan' team). The Milan team were influenced by Gregory Bateson's (1972) groundbreaking ideas about complex interpersonal communication processes. Indeed, Bateson's ideas have not yet been superseded. It is interesting that Bateson and the later Wittgenstein (whom Pearce (1995) describes as one of social constructionists' 'new' ancestors), concur on the way that 'mind' is socially constructed. The Milan team elegantly translated Bateson's systemic thinking into an inspired set of practices: hypothesising, circularity and neutrality. Cecchin transformed the latter into 'curiosity' (1987) then 'irreverence' (1992). I explore all these concepts including the crucial 'positive/logical connotation' in detail in Chapters 5, 6 and 7.

'One of the enduring contributions of systemic thinking' write Dallos and Draper (2000) in their excellent overview of systemic family therapy, 'has been to offer a view of problems . . . as fundamentally interpersonal' (p. 23). In systemic thinking relationships are the prime focus since all aspects of our social lives, such as our 'personality', are seen to be co-created through conversations and communication processes with other people. And, since cultural and societal values are translated through the family (or an equivalent) throughout our most impressionable years, these relationships and stories are seen as powerfully influential; and systemic therapists are fascinated by these unique stories. However, often what is a 'normal' (albeit complex) transition in a family creates challenges, which can (but need not) have long-term repercussions.

If, for example, a daughter who has had a close relationship with her father begins to hang out with what he sees as 'unsuitable' friends when she reaches adolescence, her father may try to persuade her not to see them. However, she might resent this. Their relationship may become volatile: he might describe her as 'difficult'; she might describe him as 'controlling'. The girl's relationship with her mother may also be affected.

A systemic therapist would be interested in the *meanings* each person gives for other people's behaviour and all their interactions: how each person responds to each other person. Asking the client to respond as if the other person is in the room gives the therapist important information about all their positions (even though the client may sometimes only guess at their answers). The therapist sees no one position as definitive (even their own) and the Milan team urged therapists not to 'fall in love with' one idea, 'hypothesis' or story.

Each person is born into a cluster of 'stories' including the political, economic and cultural zeitgeist as well as personal, family and community obligations. And systemic therapists honour all these contexts with the acronym GRRAACCCES: gender, race, religion, (differing) abilities, age, culture, colour, class, ethnicity and sexual orientation (Burnham 1992: 24). We take all these issues (and many others) into account in order to understand what affects a person's unique position in the world.

Post-Milan therapists embrace constructionism

Boscolo and Cecchin and other 'post-Milan' systemic practitioners embraced social constructionist thinking in the early to mid-1980s. Social constructionism arose from an explosion of ideas in communication and social sciences that questioned the possibility of objectivity, knowledge, reason, authority and progress in our social worlds (Gergen 2001: p. 1). Along the way many systemic therapists espoused constructivism, which sees communication as a cognitive process of knowing (foregrounding perception) (Pearce 1995), whereas constructionists (inspired by Bateson, American pragmatism and the later Wittgenstein) see communication as a social process of creating the world (foregrounding action) (Pearce 1995: p. 98).

There are many different versions of social constructionism says Pearce (1995). Not itself a unified 'theory', with no precise definition, we are still in 'uncharted seas' (p. 89). However, most versions concur with the idea that there is 'no preverbal, objective reality that we can know' (p. 97) and that we co-construct the world through language (verbal and non-verbal). Indeed, we cannot even make truth claims about social constructionism itself, or we fall into the same trap that we are trying to get out of (Lang 2004).

Pearce has devised a model with three axes along which he positions various social constructionist theorists (p. 93). Two 'realist' positions are Harré's and Shotter's: Harré, he says, suggests that we live within an *umwelt* (worldview) 'which contains moral and interpretative as well as physical events and objects, within which our actions within the *umwelt* are real. They affect as well as being affected by the moral and physical ecologies in which they occur' (p. 96). Gergen argues that *everything* is created through discourse: 'once we attempt to articulate what there is we enter the world of discourse' (Gergen 1990: 171). On the other hand Pearce positions himself, Shotter and Cronen as being 'primarily interested in foregrounding the actions (conjoint, unfinished) by which we make things real' (p. 97), what Shotter (1989, 1985, 1993) has described as 'joint action'. Shotter, he says, sees the social world as inherently fluid, meanings are always emergent; words are tools and instruments and have *a use only in a context*.

This is essentially an international oral community says Pearce (1990), drawing on Ong (1982), in which ideas are debated in ongoing conversations, rather than one in which gurus develop their theories alone, which their acolytes follow.

Language creates reality

'Effective (social constructionist) therapy' say Gergen and Warhus (in Gergen 2001):

> may ... require the use of many speech genres ... from psychoanalytic, behaviour modification, cognitive ... (it may) include spiritual discourse ... the

discourses of romance, New Age, Marxism, Zen Buddhism... The skilled therapist in a constructionist mode might be as much at home speaking the language of the street, the locker room, or the nightclub as mastering the nuances of Lacanian anaytics.' (p. 99)

Systemic therapists prefer to ask questions, which invite a client to answer from their own experience and *tell the therapist* about the *client's* worldview, in preference to making statements or giving interpretations, which *tell the client* what the *practitioner* knows. However, a therapist may decide to make a statement, give an appropriate self-disclosure and even (horror of horrors) give information or advice if this is done within a systemic frame.

But it is not the case that all 'grammars' are equally valid. Following Wittgenstein, systemic therapists claim that our language actually *creates* the kinds of people we are and the culture and society in which we live (even if we are not talking within earshot of the client) and 'rhetorical responsibility' reminds us of this (McNamee and Gergen 1999). We must become rhetorically sensitive says Pearce (1994) and self-aware. By contrast 'rhetorically insensitive' people 'act "naturally"', not... taking into account the situation... the way their acts intermesh with those of other people' (p. 326). If this makes us self-conscious and uncomfortable at times, then so be it. Anderson (1992) condemns the practice of professionals who use respectful language with clients but 'nasty' language privately. Some early systemic therapists misunderstood the process of co-creating hypotheses with other therapists and believed that 'anything goes'. But Lang (2004) says that when he hears therapists using abhorrent language when they are talking about clients, he will stop the conversation immediately.

Throughout the text I have tried to use respectful language. 'Client' implies a contractual arrangement, which is appropriate and I use 'client', 'person' and the plural 'people' interchangeably. I use the term 'therapist' throughout, although in some contexts a practitioner may be described as a counsellor, a social worker and so on. Sometimes I use the feminine pronoun when referring to a therapist. I describe therapeutic conversations as 'therapy', although these may be called 'counselling' (or some other term) in some contexts.

The examples I use throughout the text are drawn from conversations with clients; in all cases I have altered all identifying features, or have amalgamated two or more conversations to illustrate an idea. Following Epston and White (1992), these examples are 'glossed'; they do not represent the 'disorderly process of therapy – the ups and downs of that adventure that we refer to as therapy. There is a simplicity reflected in these accounts that cannot be found in the work itself' (p. 110).

The chapters

Every chapter uses examples from practice to illustrate the ideas, 'theories' and concepts.

Chapter 2 is an overview of systemic ideas, specifically Gregory Bateson's, his influence on the original Milan team and the Milan team's move towards social constructionism.

Chapter 3 explores systemic social constructionist approaches to emotion and the self. I also look at the effects of 'position' and the way that wider economic/political contexts affect a person's 'personal' (identity and family) stories.

In Chapter 4 I explore the concept of 'context', which lies at the heart of both systemic and social constructionist approaches and shows that 'reality' is always context dependent.

Chapter 5 is the first of three chapters that explore the Milan team's interrelated concepts 'hypothesising, circularity and neutrality'. This chapter explores the important stance of 'neutrality', which was critiqued and led to various transformations: 'curiosity' and 'irreverence', which enable us to question our prejudices and taken-for-granted assumptions so that therapists can become more self-reflexive and self–other-reflexive.

Chapter 6 explores the important concept of 'circularity', based on Bateson's work with 'feedback' and 'cybernetics', which the Milan team transformed into their elegant 'technique' of circular (relationship) questioning, which metaphorically includes important other people in the client's life in our therapeutic conversations.

Chapter 7 describes the process of 'hypothesising' or 'systemic story creation' to show how therapists can question our own hunches, ideas and theories before, during and after each conversation with a client. Traditionally systemic (family) therapists work in a small team or with a colleague in order to create multiple descriptions, so unaccompanied systemic therapists must find other creative ways to do this.

Chapter 8 shows how working with a person's future hopes and dreams, taking an appreciative approach and spotting a person's abilities, rather than their deficiencies can have a powerfully positive effect on the stories clients tell about themselves, their life and their relationships with others. This approach is tremendously energising for client and therapist alike.

Chapter 9 describes how 'tracking an episode' (a small piece of action or interaction) with a client can help us connect with various aspects such as a client's relationships, self-identity and other relevant stories such as culture, gender and so on. When we work with the minutiae of the person's story we respect the uniqueness of their story, connect with family and cultural stories (amongst others) and begin to notice aspects that may have been overlooked.

Chapter 10 illustrates some of the ways in which therapists can work ethically with the complex issue of change, to respect the client's wishes, and not have a secret agenda about ways in which we want them to change. I describe the way the work affects our own lives and how therapists' own stories change.

My hope is that you will enjoy reading this book and experimenting with some of these ideas in your practice. More importantly, my dream is that your clients benefit from yet more co-creative therapeutic conversations with you. I look forward to your responses.

2
OVERVIEW OF SYSTEMIC THERAPY: THEORY/PRACTICE

A systemic approach can liberate us from trying to 'get it right'
Dallos and Draper (2000)

The concept of feedback, can give a simpler and more consistent explanation of psychological data, than does the psychical energy model
Bowlby (1971)

In this chapter I give a brief overview of some of the ideas that created systemic practices, specifically Milan and post-Milan approaches. Systemic thinking created a profound shift from an individual to an interpersonal perspective. This, say Dallos and Draper (2000) 'helped liberate individuals from the oppressive and pathologising frameworks that had predominated' (p. 23).

The Milan team were profoundly influenced by Gregory Bateson (1972), British-born anthropologist and ethnologist, living in California, who provided 'the intellectual foundation' for systemic family therapy write Dallos and Draper (p. 19), and who continues to provide inspiration to succeeding generations of systemic therapists.

Kim was worried about her mother Martha, a 53-year-old white British woman, who had recently become listless and often cried for 'no reason'. Kim knew of a local Women's Centre that offered (systemic) therapy and her mother agreed to go.

Bateson studied human patterns of communication, drawing on anthropology and ethnology (the way that animals, people and the environment interact). He translated concepts from physics, engineering and biology about 'feedback' and 'cybernetics' and applied them to human interaction.

The therapist immediately begins to explore the communication patterns in Martha's life: how she had got the idea to come to talk to someone. 'Kim thinks I'm depressed.' Martha said she had been feeling low for some time and 'not her usual self'. 'Who else has noticed?' the therapist asked. Martha's husband had called her 'lazy'.

Following Bateson, the Milan team tried to make sense of the 'ecology' of the system: how everything fits together, the meanings that everybody (in the client's life) gives for each other's actions and the communication 'patterns' that have evolved.

Martha and her husband Terry have had a good 20-year-long marriage: he has a small building firm and they had fostered many children. Their daughter Kim had enjoyed being part of a large flexible family yet felt special. About a year ago she had moved into her own flat and they had decided to stop fostering. It had become too physically demanding for Martha and Terry wanted a more relaxed home life. However, at a time when they should have been reaping the rewards she had 'spoiled it all' by 'getting depressed'.

'What has made Kim describe you as depressed?' the therapist asked. 'Kim blames her dad — he's too pernickety.' Now that there were no children around he expected to come home to an immaculate home. Martha had tried to by-pass his criticisms by ensuring that the place was spotless, but she never seemed to achieve his high standards. She had felt miserable and began to 'give up'.

Over several sessions, Martha began to notice their communication 'patterns': the more Terry criticised what she had not done, the more she responded by being unable to get on with anything. The more she failed to do what Terry saw as the 'simple' job of keeping the place clean and tidy, the more frustrated he became. He tried to 'help' by telling her to 'just get on with it'; she responded by crying.

As Watzlawick et al. (1967) write, 'it can be seen time and again that a symptom that has remained refractory to psychotherapy ... suddenly reveals its significance when seen in the context of the ongoing marital interaction of the individual and his or her spouse' (p. 45).

Rather than searching for an initial 'cause', or 'reason' for Martha's low feelings and behaviour, the therapist tried to make sense of the way Martha and Terry communicated.

In this example, for clarity, I show how a therapist worked with the 'simple' communication 'patterns' between two people, who happened to be married. But of course there are often many more relevant people in a client's life, therefore even more complex communication 'patterns'.

There was another important person in Martha and Terry's life: their daughter Kim. She had noticed her mother's low mood, heard her father's critical comments and 'blamed' him. She had, Martha said, shouted at him 'Stop being so horrible to mum.' He had felt that they were 'ganging up on him' and shouted back. Their previously loving relationships became vitriolic. The antagonistic atmosphere upset Martha, who wanted a peaceful home: she became even more miserable.

Often there are many influential people involved: grandparents, people who are no longer alive, other members of the extended family, important people in the religious community, significant professionals and/or colleagues. However, relationships with members of the family are often the most passionate, since these are the ones that provide our idea of 'normality', our values, sense of self and view of the world, even if we spend the rest of our lives challenging them.

Feedback and early systemic thinking

From the outset 'cybernetics', and the concept of feedback, were fundamental to the development of systems thinking. These ideas enabled therapists to move away from an intrapsychic view of the person to an interpersonal one and helped family therapists to make sense of puzzling and repetitive communication patterns (Hoffman 1981; Jones 1993: p. 20). The idea of feedback, that we affect, and are profoundly affected by, other people, was once a revolutionary one. But it is one that we now take for granted.

The ways that Terry expressed his desire for a tidier home (now that there were no children around) provided 'feedback' to Martha. Martha's reactions (lack of interest in the home and crying) were communications to Terry; they provided 'feedback' to him. Terry's reactions (suggesting that Martha just 'get on with it') provided 'feedback' to her. Later Kim responded to the behaviour of both her mother and her father, offering 'feedback' to both of them. And so it went on.

The concept of feedback was created during the famous Josiah Macy Foundation conferences in the 1940s, where leading scientists, engineers, mathematicians and social scientists developed far-reaching ideas in communication and control. Norbert Weiner (1961, 1967) coined the term 'cybernetics' (from the Greek word for the person who steers the boat) to show that 'systems' are complex and 'self-regulating'. Two well-known examples of feedback systems using cybernetic principles are: (a) the way that a central heating system shuts off when a certain temperature is reached; (b) the way that the human body constantly regulates body temperature so that it stays at roughly 98.6°F despite external change.

In the 1950s Bateson was profoundly influenced by debates with Weiner about cybernetics and feedback at the Josiah Macy Jr conferences, but he was one of the first to suggest that feedback creates and maintains patterns of interactions between *people*. 'Rather than focussing on how one event or action causes another ... it is more appropriate to think of people as mutually generating jointly constructed patterns of actions based on continual processes of change' (Dallos and Draper 2000: p. 32).

However one therapist may 'notice' a 'pattern' of interaction between Martha, Terry and Kim, whilst another 'notices' something entirely different.

'Feedback' is not mechanistic; people co-create meanings within ever-evolving interactions and fast-moving conversations, therefore misunderstandings may develop as each person responds to what they *think* the other person 'means' by what they say and do.

Bateson pulled together a distinguished research team in Palo Alto. California in the early 1950s to study patterns and paradoxes in human and animal communication; this became the famous Mental Research Institute (known as MRI). They critiqued individual psychoanalytic work, which they said could create an escalation of problems and had even, in one case, led to suicide (Jackson 1957). Jay Hayley, John Weakland, Paul Watzlawick and Don Jackson studied communication in families where one member had a diagnosis of 'schizophrenia' (a much broader diagnosis than 'schizophrenia' in Britain today).

Bateson (1972) writes that whilst 'Freudian psychology expanded the concept of mind inwards to include communication systems within the body ... What I am saying expands mind outwards' (p. 461). 'The cybernetic epistemology ... would suggest a new approach. The individual mind is ... also in pathways and messages outside the body' (p. 275).

The therapist explored Martha's miserable feelings in relation to pathways, messages, invitations and patterns of communications between her, her husband and their daughter. Eventually they began to make sense of the way her crying and lethargy were communications that came to be described as 'depression' by her daughter and 'laziness' by Terry.

This interpersonal approach, Bateson (1972) writes, shows that medical and psychological descriptions 'cease to be matters of "minds" whose boundaries no longer coincide with the skins of the participant individuals' (p. 339). They are expressions of the relationships that people have with people in their life.

The development of family and interpersonal therapy

Because psychoanalysts at that time were banned from including relatives in sessions, as this was seen to 'contaminate' therapy, 'treatment' took place mostly in the guise of 'research'. This enabled them to work with the communication processes between people rather than with just the person showing disturbed behaviour. This emphasis on the interpersonal nature of problems 'presented a profound and significant challenge to the existing psychiatric orthodoxy' and 'was liberating not only for families . . . but also for the therapist' (Dallos and Draper 2000: p. 21). Early systemic therapists preferred to work with couples and family members but if we use what Bateson called 'systemic wisdom', we can bring the voices of important other people into the room when we work systemically with an individual.

The therapist asked Martha to imagine what Terry and Kim might reply, if they were there. This brought them metaphorically into the room, and helped to make sense of their interactions and what they were co-creating together.

Experimental psychology did work with interpersonal contexts, say Watzlawick et al. (1969), but unfortunately, the language of psychology (and the way research is conducted) does not reflect this. For example, in psychology a concept (such as depression) is studied 'as if it were a measurable quantity in the human mind', so that eventually the construct ('depression') becomes reified as a *thing* possessed by people rather than 'a shorthand expression for a particular form of ongoing relationship' (p. 27).

The therapist did not talk about Martha's 'depression' (or her 'laziness') in a way that quantified them or as if they were 'real things' each with an independent existence of their own (or resided inside her), but explored how these descriptions come to be made about her. What would Terry say (if he were there) had made him use the word 'lazy' about Martha? What was he was trying to communicate by saying this? How does this affect Martha?

Words like 'laziness', 'depression', 'dependency' 'hostility', 'love' and so on are seen as verbal descriptions of the way we are communicating (behaving) with other people; they are simply *descriptions*. To say that they are 'real things' that people 'express' as 'messages' to other people is the wrong way round Bateson says (p. 275).

When Terry calls Martha 'lazy' this communication may profoundly affect her; but the word does not refer to an inherent quality of 'laziness' that she possesses. This is simply Terry's way of describing her actions, which are different from the energetic way she used to act when the house was full of children. Similarly, when Kim says her mother 'is depressed', this is simply a description for her mother's actions (crying and not doing the housework).

At the same time the descriptions we use actually establish, constitute and create any relationship we have with another person, as Bateson points out.

Even if Martha describes herself as 'depressed' the therapist would explore the meanings of this description, when and where (in which contexts) and with whom she came to describe herself in this way. And what effect does this have on other people?

Concepts of feedback and cybernetics influenced systemic therapists' preference for asking questions rather than mainly reflecting back, summarising, making statements and interpretations and so on. Questions allow therapists to *learn* about the *client's* meanings, their feelings, thoughts and actions and help make sense of their interaction. On the other hand, statements *tell* the client what the *therapist* thinks and feels.

The 'quiet revolution' in Milan

Using 'general systems theory' a host of therapists had begun to do family therapy in America and Britain in the late 1950s and the 1960s. But it was in Italy in 1968, that a 'quiet revolution' was taking place says Hoffman (1981) The 'ideas of the Bateson group leaped across an ocean and took root in Italian soil' (p. 284). Mara Selvini Palazzoli, discouraged by her results with anorectic children and impressed by the Palo Alto group's writings, set up the Centre for Study of the Family. By 1971 four psychoanalysts were developing systemic ideas and practices: Selvini herself, Giuliana Prata (another woman), Luigi Boscolo and Gianfranco Cecchin (two men). Called the Milan Associates, they invited Watzlawick from Palo Alto to consult to them and over the next ten years worked together for two days a week seeing families. Often they were able to transform families where one member had a diagnosis of anorexia or 'schizophrenia' in just ten sessions where other forms of treatment had failed. In 1975 they returned to Bateson's original work. 'Compared to the Palo Alto approaches ... the systemic view of Bateson's original writings seemed both purer and more complex' write Boscolo and Bertrando (1996: 85). It 'opened up new horizons. ... Our thinking changed radically and became more complex'. They developed their unique Milan systemic approach. They translated Bateson's ideas into a 'brilliantly articulated ... set of practices' (Pearce 1994: p. 236). I describe their three principles, hypothesising, circularity and neutrality in Chapters 5, 6 and 7 and another important concept, the 'positive/logical connotation', below.

From 'linear' energy systems to 'systemic information' systems

As noted, Bateson's ideas enabled the Milan team to shift from a psychoanalytic to a systemic orientation. They built on his key distinction between:

(1) science and physics, in which energy systems are based on cause-and-effect;
(2) the world of communication, in which information systems are based on stimulus-response/response-stimulus in an ongoing circular process.

In the scientific world of matter, Bateson (1972) writes, 'When one billiard ball strikes another there is an *energy transfer,* the second ball is *energized* by the impact of the first.' This linear cause-and-effect model is much like the medical model where an infection is said to *cause* an inflammation (Watzlawick et al. 1967: p. 214). However, this model does not work with human (and animal) communication.

Bateson used two more analogies to compare the two approaches:

(1) if a person kicks a *stone,* the trajectory (created by the *energy forces* involved) is *predictable*;

(2) if a person kicks a *dog*, (because the kick is a *communication*, a way of giving *information*) *we can never predict* how the dog will interpret this information, nor how it will *react*.

The dog might bite, bark, whimper and cower or run away. Also, we can never predict how the *person* will react to the *dog's reactions* and so on. 'In communication systems' Bateson (1972) writes, 'the *energy* of the response is usually provided by the *respondent*. If I kick a dog, his immediate sequential behaviour is energized by his metabolism, not by my kick' (p. 403). And the dog's metabolism will limit the number of responses it is likely to make. Of course, we humans have a much wider array of responses from which to choose, but they will not be limitless.

It would be impossible to predict how Martha might feel after they stopped fostering, or after Kim had left home, nor how Terry might respond to their new way of living.

It is interesting that Bowlby (1971), writing from an Object Relations perspective, also critiqued the way that a model from physics was imported into psychotherapy. He quotes Freud (1953–74) in order to critique him: 'We assume as other natural sciences have led us to expect, that in mental life *some kind of energy is at work*' (my emphasis) (pp. 163–4). 'This model is an attempt to view human and psychological information in the same ways as those of the physics and chemistry current in the second half of the 19th century' says Bowlby (pp. 14–15). But in fact these ideas 'soon became discredited even within the scientific community' he says.

Martha told the therapist that she was frustrated, upset and angry with Terry and this maelstrom of feelings was making her feel confused. She shared Terry's wish for a tidy home, but wanted him to understand that at the moment this was too difficult. In any case after many years of domesticity this was not her top priority.

There are two major ways in which Bowlby echoes systemic thinking:

(1) the individual has a 'strong tendency to seek relationships with other persons' (p. 16);
(2) 'the concept of feedback, can give a simpler and more consistent explanation of psychological data, than ... the psychical energy model' (p. 20).

The therapist helped Martha find ways to give Terry sensitive but clear verbal feedback on how his behaviour was affecting her. This was not easy and one time she became so frustrated that she 'gave him an earful'. He was shocked; she was sorry. But he heard.

'The concept of feedback is crucial' write Selvini et al. (1978: p. 5), and 'we must abandon the causal-mechanistic view of phenomena, which has dominated the sciences until recent times and adopt a systemic orientation.'

The therapist noticed that as Martha began to communicate more directly to her husband he became a little less critical and she cried less often. As Terry understood Martha more and recognised how his behaviour was affecting her, he found himself not needing to give her 'feedback' (through criticism) about her 'laziness'. She, in turn, realised how much he had been looking forward to a childfree, tidier home.

The Milan team's distinct systemic orientation was an 'extremely elegant, complex' approach (which) continually evolved' say Dallos and Draper (2000: p. 80). However, because of the profound ideological differences between Bateson's systemic orientation and Jay Hayley's (1976) 'strategic' stance that 'proposed that at the heart of the psychotherapeutic process was a struggle for control', their early writings were confused say Boscolo et al. (1987: pp. 5–6). Whilst their publications brought them huge acclaim, their early language was adversarial. But their term 'game', by which they meant logic, was misunderstood. And further misunderstandings arose when enthusiastic practitioners used the notion of the 'paradox' in simplistic non-systemic ways, or tried to import systemic practices into organisations not ready for them.

The 'tyranny of linguistic conditioning'

The Milan team changed their way of talking with, and about, clients when they read Shands' (1971) critique of 'the tyranny of linguistic conditioning' (p. 32). Shands observes that European language creates the assumption that there is a 'linear' causality in our ordinary life. Language demands subject and object, actor and acted upon, a before and after, and we conclude 'that the universe is organised on a linear basis, in cause and effect patterns'. We 'are imprisoned by the absolute incompatibility between the two primary systems in which the human being lives; the living system, dynamic and circular, and the symbolic system (language), descriptive, static, and linear' (Selvini et al. 1978: p. 52).

Terry had called Martha 'lazy' 'because' when he came home he saw unwashed dishes in the sink and Martha lying on the sofa surrounded by magazines. But this creates the assumption that Martha's actions (and non-actions) caused Terry's annoyance in a 'linear' (unicausal) way.

It is the way we use language that creates the idea of 'cause and effect', or 'linear' descriptions. These then become the everyday way to look at the world, says Shands. In a systemic orientation one-way causality is contested, since no event or any one person's behaviour is seen to *cause* the behaviour of other people. We 'were able to realise' say Boscolo et al. (1987) 'how much our belonging to a verbal world conditions us ... We conceptualise reality (whatever that may be) according to the linguistic model which thus becomes for us the same thing as reality. But language is not reality' (p. 52).

Terry might say that Martha's behaviour 'made him' criticise her 'because' he was fed-up with coming home after a hard day's work to a messy house. Martha might say that she 'couldn't be bothered' to do anything round the house 'because' whatever she does is 'not good enough' for Terry. Kim might say that she shouted at her father 'because' he was so nasty to her mother.

Each of these statements is a linear (causal) explanation. Linear thinking is normal and useful as a starting place, but explanations of this kind tend to terminate dialogue and conversations. 'When we assume that we have an explanation, we often give up looking for other descriptions' (Cecchin 1987: 406).

If Martha's therapist follows the 'linear' idea that Terry's criticisms are 'making' Martha feel miserable, then it could become an explanation, an end in itself and she could stop becoming curious about other ways of understanding things.

The problem is words, says Shands. 'Only with words can man [sic] become conscious ... Only through getting the better of words does it become possible for some, a little of the time, to transcend the verbal context and to become, for brief instants, free' (pp. 19–20).

Martha's therapist played with many different metaphors and ideas: maybe Terry wants to become more involved in the home now that he and Martha have the place to themselves; maybe they could experiment with one week having a 'clean and tidy' home and the following week a 'messy' one?

When the possible *causes* of behaviour are given second place, write Watzlawick et al. (1967), we recognise that it is the *effect* of the behaviour that is of 'prime significance in the interaction of closely related individuals' (p. 45).

The therapist becomes curious about the effect of Martha's tears on Kim, Terry, and on herself.

Systemic therapists are encouraged to have conversations with other systemic thinkers. 'You need to confront your own linear thinking with the linear thinking of someone else' Cecchin says (in Boscolo et al. 1987). This enables one to begin to develop a more systemic and interactional orientation.

The therapist might start with the idea that 'Terry is making Martha miserable' and develop it further: 'How might things look from Terry's position?' 'How did Martha help him develop his observational skills?' and so on.

We must be careful not to create an either/or dichotomy: 'linear is bad' and 'systemic is good', since this in itself is 'not sufficiently systemic' (Pearce 1992). As Cecchin (1987) says 'we should accept linear explanations as long as we do not believe them' (p. 406).

From 'to be' to 'to show'

The Milan team (1978; 1980) used an ingenious way to avoid the 'tyranny of linguistic conditioning': they simply replaced the verb 'to be' with the verb 'to show'.

When Martha said that Terry had described her as 'lazy' the therapist asked 'If Terry were here how would he say you show laziness?' Martha replied 'He came home early the other day when I hadn't washed up. He called me a lazy cow.'

This helps the therapist to understand what Martha is *showing* to Terry that gives him the idea that she 'is lazy'. Another person may describe Martha as 'relaxed' or not even notice the unwashed dishes.

Other questions that explore the behaviour that Terry describes as 'lazy' could be 'Who else would agree that you are lazy?' 'Who would disagree?' 'What would he call untidy?' 'What would you call untidy?' 'Are you more or less untidy than you used to be?' 'What other description would Kim give for your behaviour?' 'How would your mother/best friend/sister describe what you are doing?'

These kinds of questions:

(1) help us work with interpersonal relationships and the ways people communicate;
(2) avoid the illusion that a description is a truthful account of the person's personality;
(3) show that a description about a person's behaviour is simply that: a description made by somebody;
(4) show that descriptions (such as 'laziness', 'depression' and so on) are aspects of relationships.

This is very different from seeing 'laziness' as an inherent quality that Martha possesses.

Eventually Martha and Terry developed new ways of communicating. She re-established contact with old friends and began to feel less hopeless; Terry was relieved that Martha was not becoming 'depressed'. They went on several enjoyable outings, rekindling their enjoyment of each other's company. He began to place less emphasis on a tidy home. Kim and her father began to get on better, as he and Martha became happier.

The positive/logical connotation

The positive connotation is a 'multivisioned view of problems'. It was the 'most compelling invention of the Milan team' writes Hoffman (in Boscolo et al. 1987). This idea, that no 'truth' is more true or less true than another, led to a 'new therapeutic gestalt' and was no less than a 'restructuring of therapists' consciousness' she says (p. 7).

Juliette, a 19-year-old white French woman, came to talk about how difficulties with eating were affecting her enjoyment of life. The therapist explored all the important relationships in her life, including her relationship with food. By 'positively connoting' all these relationships the therapist helped Juliette to make sense of these communications. The therapist also 'positively connoted' her behaviour (not eating) and tried to understand how this made sense. Although the therapist did not indicate that Juliette's style of eating was 'wrong' she did commiserate with her on the way this was restricting her life and was harmful to her health.

The positive connotation evolved from the Palo Alto therapists' technique of 'prescribing the symptom', but the Milan team realised that this could inadvertently 'negatively connote' other people who do not have the symptom.

For example, if the therapist condones Juliette's behaviour or suggests that she should continue to restrict her eating (to avoid blaming her), her parents and/or other family members could feel that they must be 'to blame' (if it is not Juliette's 'fault', then it must be somebody's 'fault').

This relates to the Western idea that responsibility lies with an individual person. In a systemic orientation we recognise that problems develop through a process of mutual communication: nobody is 'to blame'. A person's actions do have consequences; but we do not know how they will affect other people. 'Relational responsibility', McNamee and Gergen (1999) say shows that this is always interactional.

By positively connoting everybody involved in the 'problem' as well as their behaviours we accept 'the peculiar patterns of communication shared by all members of the family' write Selvini et al. (1978: p. 59). When we accept these patterns we 'join' the client and their 'system', and begin to appreciate things from everybody's position.

The therapist tried to appreciate the ways in which restricting her food intake may be helpful for Juliette and/or those in her life. What might Juliette want to communicate to certain people by her behaviour? Is this preferable to another way of living? Is it now difficult for her behave differently?

In a systemic orientation we work with the idea that every action is a communication and every communication is an invitation to other people to respond in some way.

How are the people in Juliette's life affected by her ways of communicating? How do they respond? What meanings does she give to their reactions? Are their communications inadvertently reinforcing her behaviour?

Of course starving oneself can be highly dangerous, as are other hurtful kinds of behaviours. So Selvini et al. (1978) asked 'Why not have a systemic orientation but say that the symptom of the identified patient and the behaviours of the family are both "wrong"?' 'Because', they answer, 'this generates pain and suffering'. And, more importantly, it implies that the system *should change because it is 'wrong'*. In this way 'one would reject that system' and 'preclude any possibility of being accepted' by those involved (p. 56).

The therapist might wonder whether Juliette is communicating something to other people that mere words would not achieve. This can be the case where sex abuse has been, or still is a part of a person's life; actions, such as self-starvation, remind others to remain vigilant.

These ideas helped the Milan team avoid 'the dangers that follow in the wake of blame/guilt ... violence, scapegoating, somatizing ...': no-one can change (easily) under a negative connotation (Boscolo et al. 1987).

Juliette gives important information: her parents have had a tempestuous marriage but are now united in encouraging her to eat. Maybe her struggle with food is a way of creating a focus for her parents? Maybe as they pull together, they put their plans to divorce on hold? Maybe they demonstrate to Juliette that she is more important than their own individual happiness? Maybe by not eating Juliette is keeping the family together?

Using the positive connotation is no mere technique says Jones (1993), since the therapist strives to understand everybody and 'make sense of behaviour which otherwise would seem to be insane or malicious' (p. 17). It helps us understand actions that may at first seem unwanted, 'bizarre' or 'crazy'. The Milan therapists often did become indignant and angry with clients or, for example the parents of a client, Selvini et al. (1978) write, but the positive connotation helped them to think and work systemically (p. 176).

However, this concept was problematic says Jones, since it implied that 'disturbing behaviours were functional or good or that the family needed such a symptom' (p. 18). So the Milan team developed the 'logical connotation': therapists seek to understand how certain actions have become habitual and/or are meaningful in the context.

What is logical about the way Juliette and her parents behave? When did she start to restrict her food intake? If she says that dieting helped her become slim so she could fit into the 'in-crowd' at school and avoid being bullied for being overweight, we could ask whether it had become a habit that she is now afraid to stop. Maybe it has become her 'friend'?

Understanding the *logic* of each person's responses to 'the problem' and so on enables the therapist to make sense of how that particular logic evolved within that set of relationships.

If Juliette says that her mother started phoning her more often when she realised how thin Juliette had become, the therapist may be curious about what ideas her mother has about Juliette's behaviour. If Juliette views this as interfering, the therapist may wonder whether this is the way her mother shows her concern. How does Juliette respond to her mother's more frequent phone calls? Has their relationship become closer, or is it less close?

But it is useful to retain the idea of the 'positive connotation' to help us to put into practice the maxim that 'everybody is doing the best they can, given all the circumstances.' We 'look into the negative for the moral/logical connotation' says Lang (2004). However bizarre the communications and behaviour, our job is to make sense of things from the positions of *all* the relevant people.

Maybe Juliette's body also has a voice? What would it say if it could speak?

We are all embodied and long-term nutritional deficiencies can affect us physiologically and emotionally (Holford 2003). In this way we challenge the Western assumption of a mind-body split.

Also, we explore the possible effects should the 'symptom' disappear to help to make sense of the 'logic' of the 'problem'.

The therapist could ask Juliette 'If you were to eat normally, what would life be like?' 'What things would you do that you are not doing now if you were to be free of your problem?' 'What would your parents do?'

The positive/logical connotation is invaluable when we work systemically with an individual, since there is a temptation to 'side with' the person in front of us or highlight their shortcomings whilst ignoring others people's legitimate points of view (and/or possibly to 'side with' others). It enables us to understand the *systemic* logic of the client's 'problem' (the way people co-construct their meanings and actions in ongoing communications), so that we can begin to understand, respect and appreciate the feelings, meanings and actions of *everyone* involved in the issues the client brings.

Fewer meetings can be more effective

The Milan team initially offered families weekly appointments. But when they discovered that families from southern Italy, who could only come on a monthly basis, changed more radically than families from Milan or northern Italy, who could come every week, they lengthened the interval between sessions. They would often resist a family's pleas to meet sooner, trusting the process to enable the family to create new ways of relating to each other. Intervals of a fortnight, three weeks or a month have become a feature of systemic work. Sometimes a therapist has very few conversations with a person over a long period of time, giving systemic therapy the description 'brief-long' therapy.

At the end of the conversation we usually discuss with the client when next to meet (or even whether a further session is needed): we respect the client's opinion about the best timescale for conversations. However, we do not preclude weekly meetings, as a week can seem an extremely long time for certain clients. And a therapist may 'persuade' the client to meet sooner (if for example they are suicidal). But this is done through open negotiation. However, if a less vulnerable client assumes that they *must* have weekly meetings, the therapist may take the opportunity to explain the rationale and possible effects of longer gaps which can:

- demonstrate that the client is the expert in their life;
- enable the client to focus on their relationships with important others and their life, rather than on the therapist–client relationship;
- encourage the client to develop resources and resolve difficulties with important others;
- enable the client to choose whether to use (or ignore) any new ideas and/or connections made in the therapeutic conversation;
- give time for other people to respond to any changes that the client makes;

- allow time for the client to respond to other people's responses, and so on;
- mean that the client owns any changes they make in their life, rather than attributing them to the therapist/therapy;
- strengthen the client's relationships with important other people in their life, rather than with the therapist;
- make therapy less costly for clients (if they are paying);
- be cost-effective for agencies as therapists are able to handle a much larger caseload.

Second-order cybernetics

'Second-order cybernetics' represents a radical, but gradual, shift in position for the therapist. Contrasted with the 'first-order cybernetic' position where the therapist assumes a position of 'expert', the 'second-order' therapist is more like a 'collaborative explorer' co-creating meanings with the client. In the earlier position the therapist is rather like 'a scientist who was seen to be able to accurately diagnose the problems in the family, identify the functions that symptoms were serving and intervene to alter these so that the unhealthy function that the symptoms were serving could be remedied' (Dallos and Draper 2000: p. 66).

A therapist taking a 'first-order cybernetic' position with Juliette would work solely with her stories and interactions with the important people in her life, largely negating their influence on the therapeutic conversation (and vice versa).

By contrast, a therapist taking a 'second-order cybernetic' position appreciates that as soon as we meet a person we inevitably affect, and are affected by, them. As Bateson (1972) says, we are always and inevitably a part of any 'ecology' (or system) we meet. Taking a more social constructionist position we recognise that our own personal and professional stories enable us to notice certain 'patterns', whilst ignoring others. And we inevitably influence the conversation through the language we use, our responses, what we 'see' and 'hear', notice or do not notice. These idea were present in Bateson et al.'s (1956) earlier work say Dallos and Draper. What we hear in any communication 'is in part determined by what we expect and want to hear . . . by the history of the relationship (and by the) . . . context' (Watzlawick 1964: p. 66). In this way therapist and client co-create 'reality' in the conversation between them.

If Juliette's therapist asks her what she had eaten since they last met this expands the idea that food intake is important. If, on the other hand, the therapist explores Juliette's hopes for the future, this co-creates other feelings, thoughts and ideas.

Neither focus is 'right' or 'wrong'. But each is based on a particular set of ideas. Boscolo and Cecchin's oft-quoted mantra that therapists must not 'fall in love with' their hypotheses is a way of taking a second-order position. At a micro level the different utterances that the therapist makes *will* co-create different kinds of stories and a different 'reality' for the client. So we must notice the effect on the client of the words, concepts, and metaphors we use, the questions we ask and the comments and statements we make (and our gestures and facial expressions).

Boscolo and Cecchin develop their 'post-Milan' approach

In the late 1970s Boscolo and Cecchin, the two men in the Milan team, began travelling around the world demonstrating and teaching systemic family therapy, and split off from the original Milan team. Their 'post-Milan' systemic approach remained consistent with Batesonian systemic thinking, yet constantly evolved in response to conversation with families, trainees and practitioners. For example they addressed critiques of 'neutrality', developed 'curiosity', questioned prejudice and introduced 'irreverence' (Cecchin 1987; Cecchin et al. 1992). Their innovative practices developed in ways that are congruent with social constructionist thinking. They have, inevitably, attracted criticism, but Dallos and Draper say 'some extreme critiques and rejections of these ideas, such as Anderson and Goolishian's (1988), can . . . be seen to be based on a distorted, oversimplified and mechanistic vision of (systemic) . . . theory. This can make for neat and tidy arguments but may not do justice to and represent the depth and complexity of the original ideas' (p. 66). 'Boscolo and Cecchin opened up pathways we are still exploring and developing' write Lang and McAdam (1997: 12) in the edition of the journal *Human Systems* dedicated to 25 years of the post-Milan team's influence on systemic therapy. Those of us who have observed the agility, subtlety, grace, humility and beguiling ease of Boscolo and Cecchin's therapeutic work are fortunate indeed.

Systemic ideas

- We are immersed in communication, in every way we *are* the communication.
- Every communication is an invitation.
- People are primarily influenced by relationships.
- People mutually influence each other through interaction processes.
- The concept of feedback (and 'information') makes better sense than causality.
- People respond in diverse and unpredictable ways.
- Living systems are dynamic and circular (systemic), whilst European languages are 'linear'.
- The verb 'to show' helps us work with interactional processes (unlike the verb 'to be').
- An 'ecological' model suggests that people (and everything in the world) are mutually influential.
- Descriptions (such as 'dependency', 'depression', 'love' and so on) are communications, not 'real things'.
- 'Positively/logically connoting' the client, significant others (and their 'symptoms') enables clients to feel understood and avoids blame.
- When we meet a client we become inextricably involved in their meaning system.
- The therapist's ways of viewing the world, our talk and ways of acting powerfully affect the therapeutic conversation and the client.
- Longer intervals between meetings can create change more quickly than more frequent ones and minimise dependency on the therapist.

3
SOCIAL CONSTRUCTIONIST APPROACHES TO EMOTION AND THE SELF

Let the use of words teach you their meaning
                                        Wittgenstein (1953)
Language is the most powerful tool that humans have ever invented
                                        Pearce (1994)

In this chapter I explore some inspirational aspects of systemic social constructionist practice:

(1) feelings and emotion;
(2) the 'self' and identity;

and more briefly:

(3) 'position' and our right to speak;
(4) social, cultural and economic factors.

Boscolo and Cecchin (the post-Milan team) began sharing their rigorous and imaginative ideas with practitioners around the world in the late 1970s and embraced social constructionist ideas.

Around the mid-1980s 'exciting developments in ethnomethodology... feminist social science' and so on 'burst across the sundry disciplines of science and the humanities... (stirring) enormous controversy' says Gergen (2001: p. ix). Questioning the 'positivistic' paradigm in the social sciences, these 'social constructionist' dialogues created very different ways of thinking, talking and acting; and they have now entered the mainstream (p. 1).

Social constructionism suggests that meanings are socially constructed within ordinary conversations. And feelings, emotions, the self and all aspects of our social worlds are culturally and historically constructed. We share some meanings with others of our gender and culture, but there may be other more relevant 'local' meanings/stories that have developed within our particular family or personal experiences.

However, we do not aim to create a universal or 'new foundation for therapy', write Gergen and Warhus (2001), since this is precisely what these approaches challenge. A unitary theory that holds true in every place and every historical context would be 'antithetical to social constructionist dialogues . . . (as this would) freeze cultural meaning . . . across time, circumstances and context of interpretation' (p. 97). Indeed constructionist thinkers even question the traditional notion that 'theory' precedes action. Cronen (2000), drawing on Wittgenstein, says theory does not so much *guide* what we do, but is *'meaning in use'*: theories are actually *created* within our conversations and actions (15, 25–6). A better way of talking about 'theory' says Shotter (1993) is to use Wittgenstein's idea of a 'toolbox' of concepts, ideas, skills and practices: some of which are useful in one context, some in another context.

Controversy around social constructionism continues to rage. Indeed, there is no agreement about whether to retain the term: Rom Harré (1995) prefers 'discursive psychology', Pearce (1995) describes a range of perspectives, and Bernstein (1991) talks about 'a constellation'; '. . . we can no longer . . . claim that there is or can be a final reconciliation . . . in which all difference . . . and contradiction are reconciled' (p. 8).

However, it is Wittgenstein's (1953) highly influential later work that unites those who question 'foundational', 'essentialist' and 'positivistic' approaches (Gergen 2001; Harré and Gillett 1994; Pearce 1994). Although in the *Tractatus* (1922) he attempted to 'prove' the existence of an underlying essence, Wittgenstein later made a complete about-turn, fiercely challenging this. He spent the rest of his life struggling to articulate the way *language* (verbal and non-verbal) and common agreements create meanings and 'reality'. Language, he says, plays a vast variety of tricks on us: misleading and bewitching us (Finch 1995: pp. 42–3). Wittgenstein's work shatters any illusion that a therapist can be an expert on what a client *really* means, what is going on 'inside' their 'minds'. Systemic 'constructionist' therapists explore the way language 'bewitches' us and constitutes our realities, by constantly scrutinising our own use of words and non-verbal language.

More importantly, since therapists are afforded a more powerful position in our culture, therapists' own stories and 'theories', ways of feeling, talking and acting, will have a powerful impact on the way that 'reality' gets co-constructed within the therapeutic conversation. In other words, the way we talk with clients affects how they come to describe themselves (and others).

Emotions are socially constructed

People generally come to therapy to talk about their feelings, so appreciating the complexities of emotion-talk is crucial. Radical developments in psychological research and anthropological psychology have led to a transformation in the psychology of the emotions say Harré and Gillett (1994: p. 144). Seen in our culture as internal, private, abstract, primitive, and belonging more to women than to men, all these taken-for-granted notions are now disputed.

Cheryl, a 27-year-old white British woman, went to see a GP-based systemic therapist to make sense of 'a minor breakdown'. She had 'gone mad', screaming and shouting at her husband and becoming so hysterical that she could not remember much of what she had said or done.

We are beginning to recognise that feelings and emotions, like any other aspect of our social lives, invoke *local* moral values, which we learn within our family, community, society and culture (Averill 1982, 1992; Lutz 1988; 1996; Harré and Gillett 1994; Harré and Parrott 1996).

Cheryl said she had discovered that her husband had 'cheated' on her with two of their female friends. She was shocked and ready to end the marriage. The therapist explored Cheryl's local stories about how a woman should respond to the discovery of her spouse's infidelity. Also, the family, cultural and personal identity stories that had influenced her responses.

Emotion is 'a master cultural category in the West' says Catharine Lutz (1988), in her groundbreaking study of emotions on a South Pacific island. For the past 2000 years in the West we have talked as if emotions have an inherently unchanging nature and an essence: emotions have been 'sought in the supposedly permanent structures of human existence – spleens, souls, genes, human nature and individual psychology'. But Wittgenstein challenged this (as did Rousseau to some extent), showing how emotion is 'constructed primarily by people rather than by nature' (Lutz 1988: pp. 53–4).

Cheryl had begun to search for reasons for her 'hysterical breakdown' in her early life; she wanted to remedy this 'flaw' in her personality.

In our culture we 'usually think of emotion as a physiological or intraspsychic state that happens to us' says Pearce (1994: p. 178). But Averill (1982, 1992), also following Wittgenstein, says that these ideas are embedded within the language that we use in specific situations (what Wittgenstein calls 'language games': contexts in which we use particular words, concepts and so on).

The 'language game' that Cheryl used (an explanation based on personal flaws) shows that she views her emotions as internal, individual and originating in the past.

But emotions are short-lived 'roles' that we 'play'; Averill suggests that they come into being in the interaction between actual or imagined persons in well-structured episodes and in specific situations.

During her 'hysterical outburst', Cheryl's husband had pleaded forgiveness. She had accurately conveyed the full force and strength of her shock and revulsion for his actions.

Using Averill's ideas, Cheryl was 'sending' her husband a clear 'message' that no 'calm rational' discussion would have done. He was left in no doubt about her feelings.

Cheryl had then vacated the marital bed. These communications were invitations to her husband. He had responded by being more considerate and by having individual therapy.

The way we 'do' an emotion is partly related to our gender, culture, ethnicity and so on, partly specific to the context and partly a wish for a particular kind of response. Systemic therapists are curious about the person's ideas: exploring how they came to *feel* an emotion, and *express* it in that way.

Emotions are culturally specific

Feelings and emotions invoke *local* moral values, which we learn within our family, community, society and culture (Averill 1982, 1992; Lutz 1988; 1990; 1996; Harré and Gillett 1994; Harré and Parrott 1996).

In this context (because of Cheryl's preference for personal therapy as a way of making sense of her actions) one idea is that her husband showed his emotional reaction by communicating in a way that fitted Cheryl's moral values.

Emotions are not universal, not necessarily transferable across cultures, but are culturally constructed and culturally specific. This is 'not simply a claim that emotions are universal experiences that take on cultural particularity through variation in the situations that come to elicit them' says Lutz (1988: p. 210). She quotes DeRivera: 'it would be incorrect to say that a situation causes an emotion or that an emotion causes a perception of the situation. Rather the person's situation is always interpreted *by* some emotion' which has been socially constructed within a specific language (p. 47).

Emotions are not always culturally interchangeable; for example, one of five kinds of 'anger' Lutz identified on the Pacific island was *song*, a kind of 'justifiable anger'. A person who claims *song* is referring to a violation of a taboo or law, which must be dealt with by the chiefs. It is taken seriously and shows that the speaker is 'someone with a finely tuned and mature sense of island values' (Lutz 1990: pp. 206–7). But she says, unlike 'anger' in the American context, *song* aims to restore peace and well being.

So far we have not explored Cheryl's husband's emotions. But a systemic therapist would try to understand both her and his meanings.

Emotions are historically specific

Emotions are historically specific. Even the meaning of the word 'emotion' has changed in the Western world since the 17th century. From meaning the 'agitated behaviour of a crowd ... people running around' without any reference to private individualised feelings, 'it came to mean extravagant individual behaviour of an emotional kind' and expanded to include bodily feelings say Harré and Gillett (1994). By the beginning of the 19th century 'emotions became feminised and sentimentalised. Men had rudimentary emotions or none at all' (p. 153). Of course, they continue, 'we don't know what anyone was feeling in a family fracas of 1860, but we do know the rules of use for the words they would have used to describe it.'

Some emotions, such as accidie (a familiar emotion in the 17th century meaning bitter melancholy) have disappeared. Many have altered significantly over time: grief, which seems so deep and central an emotion, has undergone several historical transformations, varies greatly from culture to culture and may even be absent in some say Stearns and Knapp (1996: 132–50). This demonstrates the degree of plasticity in human emotional nature.

How do we learn to 'do' emotions?

If we accept that emotions are socially, historically and culturally constructed we must explore the *specific* stories, communication processes and contexts in which our clients have developed their ways of feeling.

Elisabeth, a 43-year-old black woman from St Lucia, came to therapy to 'sort out her life'. She talked rapidly, telling her therapist Helen (a white British woman) that four of her six children had been put into care against her will; relatives were caring for her two youngest children. She now lived alone and was working in an office. Elisabeth showed great distress.

We learn ways of 'doing' emotions: they are not innate. Therefore we are curious about where and in which contexts a person has developed their unique ways of 'doing' particular feelings.

A story emerged in which Elisabeth, trying to make a life far from her own country and family, had been let down by 'everybody' and had tried to bring up her children under severe financial constraints. She felt overwhelmed by a sense of failure, deeply ashamed, angry at the unfairness of life, and talked of being seen as a 'bad mother'. At this point she cried.

Judgements are often made about the 'right' way to bring up a child; in Britain where the nuclear family is still the norm there is an expectation that the main caregiver will be the mother; the father is normally the main provider. These cultural and gender discourses mean that a mother is deemed to be a 'good' or a 'bad' person depending on how she brings up her child, whilst a father's behaviour does not carry the same sanctions.

Helen asked 'What's distressing you so much now?' Elisabeth continued to cry. 'Are you more distressed about the shame, the unfairness, or is it that you are missing your children? What's the strongest feeling?' Helen asked. 'I miss Rory' she sobbed. 'And I feel bad about letting him go.' Elisabeth had consented to her first child being fostered to give him a 'better chance in life' as her circumstances at the time made it difficult for her to cope. 'I'm a bad mother' she reiterated.

Helen knew that historically, because of economic pressures in the West Indies, men were not involved with childrearing as they were forced to seek work away from their wives and children. And it was normal for a grandmother, aunt, or sister to take care of a woman's child. Therefore the idea that a woman was a 'bad mother' because she could not personally care for her children may relate more to the British culture than the West Indian one.

'Who would agree (that you are a "bad mother")?' Helen asked. 'Everybody' Elisabeth said, but could not name anybody. 'Who would not agree?' Helen asked. 'My mother and Auntie Jeannie' Elisabeth said. They would call it 'bad luck' and 'circumstances'.

Emotional feelings and displays, say Harré and Gillett (1994), function as 'psychologically equivalent to statements . . . a kind of "vocabulary" of sign forms' (pp. 145–6).

Helen wondered what 'statement' (intentional or unintentional) Elisabeth's distress was making, and to whom this was a communication. But first she wanted to make sense of Elisabeth's particular story.

When we use an emotion concept this evokes a particular social interaction says Lutz; and this 'is done in particular contexts for particular ends, to negotiate aspects of social reality and to create that reality' (1988: p. 10). This is not to say that a person 'intentionally' sets out to achieve all this when they are expressing an emotion; nor, conversely, are they 'unaware' (unconscious) of their actions. It may simply be because, like the fish that does not notice the water in which it is swimming, we do not notice the many complex issues involved when we are feeling and expressing emotions.

Helen wondered about the accompanying emotions linked to Elisabeth's distress; what stories and scenarios did she connect to when she described herself as a 'bad mother'? Maybe she was demonstrating to the therapist (a white woman) that she did care about her children.

As noted, in Western culture a 'good mother' must under all circumstances continue to take care of her children. However, there may be other influential family, religious or cultural stories.

'What comes to mind when you call yourself a "bad mother"?' Helen asked. Elisabeth cried copiously, and could not speak. 'If your tears could speak,

what might they be saying?' Helen asked. *'Shame',* Elisabeth said. *'I feel ashamed.'*

To some extent emotions fulfil 'the social purposes of the person' says Pearce (1994: p. 178). What are the social purposes of Elisabeth's 'shame'? In experiential terms shame, compared to guilt, notes Demos (1996), means 'I am weak, inadequate, inferior' (p. 75). Did 'shame' have these connotations here?

'When do you feel most ashamed?' Helen asked. Elisabeth was ashamed of the unsuccessful relationships she had had with the various men who had fathered her children. Each one had eventually left and had not supported her or the child. This was useful information, but instead of exploring these relationships (which could have led to even more 'shameful' details) Helen asked 'Is this the only way you feel ashamed?' 'No', Elisabeth said; she felt deeply ashamed of having 'lost control' of the four older children who were now living with other families.

We may make the assumption that 'of course a woman would feel ashamed if she has had to give up her children,' and/or 'of course a woman who has been abandoned many times by her partners would feel ashamed.' But neither may be the case for this *particular* person. We question our taken-for-granted prejudices and explore the *specific* conversations and relationships in which a person has developed that emotion.

'Do you recall when, and how, you first felt ashamed?' Helen asked. Elisabeth remembered the first Social Services case conference, about Rory her eldest son, when she had felt 'judged' as being a deficient mother. She also recalled her older sister's scorn at the time (Elisabeth was bitter that her sister had not helped to prevent these difficulties).

Emotions are not abstract entities, say Harré and Gillett (1994), although they are often thought of as such. They are 'actual moments of emotional feelings and displays', moments in which we are 'feeling annoyed' or 'displaying our joy' in particular circumstances in a definite cultural setting (p. 146).

Helen heard the details of the case conference; now she had some idea about how the emotion of 'shame' came to be attached to Rory being fostered (and the idea that Elisabeth was a 'bad mother').

But understanding the connection is a long way from appreciating the force that emotion words have for both the speaker and the listener. The human body has the potential for being 'moved' says Lutz and 'the relationships among the physical, the mental, and the emotional are some of the thorniest tangles in our conceptual forest' (Lutz 1988: p. 9).

Now Elisabeth says, more passionately, that she was angry with the 'unfair' treatment she had suffered at the hands of Social Services who had taken three of her children away against her will. She becomes upset, talking loudly and rapidly. 'I've got so much shame and anger inside me' Elisabeth says. 'I've got to get it out.'

Lutz says that emotion words are seen in Western language as 'concretized psychophysical states or objectivized things' (Lutz 1988: p. 9). We tend to 'reify' words, to see concepts and words as *labels* for 'things'. An emotion such as 'anger' is therefore seen as an entity, a thing. This leads us to think in terms of quantity: 'how much' anger, shame or love does a person feel? Where do they feel 'it'? (in their body) and so on. Using the word 'it' indicates that an emotion has been reified.

This familiar way of talking about feelings leads us to believe that our emotions reside inside us. But, as Wittgenstein shows over and over, language 'confuses' and 'bewitches' us, which generates numerous problems. Pictures, words and grammar 'force themselves on us' (1953: nos 397, 178, 304). 'As long as there is a verb "to be" that looks at as if it functions in the same way as "to eat" and "to drink" . . . as long as we continue to talk of a river of time or an expanse of space, etc. etc., people will keep stumbling over the same puzzling difficulties and find themselves staring at something which no explanation seems capable of clearing up' (1984: 15c).

In therapeutic conversations we can attempt to overcome these confusions by exploring the *unique* context in which the person feels an emotion and uses an emotion word. And if, as Averill says, an emotion is short-lived and is linked to a unique, specific set of circumstances and relationships, it is likely that there will be other contexts in which the person does *not* feel that emotion.

'When do you feel least ashamed?' Helen asked. Elisabeth surprisingly says that she doesn't feel ashamed about sending the two younger children to live in St Lucia with relatives (to give them a better chance in life). In fact she feels proud of the way she foiled Social Services.

Therapists' own emotions are powerful

As well as exploring these discourses systemic therapists also appreciate that our feelings and emotions profoundly influence the way we listen to, and talk with, our clients.

An experienced therapist, Helen nevertheless felt overwhelmed with the abundance of details, events and people that Elisabeth kept adding to the conversation. She struggled to make sense of it all. Afterwards she felt dissatisfied with her part in the conversation.

Averill (1982, 1992), following Wittgenstein, says that the words and phrases we use when we talk about feelings actually create the way we feel. For example, when we say that we have 'fallen in love' or are 'overcome' by rage or jealousy, we imply that our feelings are not rational or intentional. And this creates reality.

Helen had made an audiotape of the conversation, which she took to supervision. As they listened they heard Elisabeth repeatedly saying that her renewed faith in God was giving her strength.

Our own feelings, emotions and stories which we connect with are crucial in what we 'hear' (and what we miss) when we listen to and talk with our clients.

'What was happening to you during the conversation?' the supervisor asked. 'What were you feeling?' Helen suddenly realised that she had been annoyed and indeed very angry with Elisabeth for her 'irresponsible behaviour', bringing numerous children into the world by different fathers and not caring for them properly. She was shocked by her strong emotions, judgmental attitude and the fact that she had been unaware of all this during the conversation. It had prevented her hearing the important information about Elisabeth's faith in God.

Now, using a method calling 'mapping personal and professional stories' (Hedges and Lang 1993) her supervisor explored the way that Elisabeth's stories had resonated with Helen's.

As the eldest girl in a large family, Helen's childhood was filled with chores. Her mother had been, to some extent, 'irresponsible' for having such a large family. When faced with a woman who had produced numerous children without taking adequate care of them, her personal story came to the fore along with powerfully visceral feelings. Helen's strong feeling of outrage had made her miss the small but significant detail that God was giving Elisabeth hope and comfort.

Emotions are discursive acts

Emotion displays are communications and discursive acts say Harré and Gillett (1994: p. 153). But in our society emotions are assumed to be non-rational 'primitive' internal states and bodily reactions to external events. A distinction is typically made between cognition (intellect) and emotion: thoughts versus feelings. But this totally misconstrues the complex role of emotions in our life and the way that bodily reactions, the social context, thoughts, meanings, 'judgements', rules/conventions, 'displays' (action), and language are all involved in the construction of emotion. In particular we must explore the local rules (conventions) of a person's feelings and emotion vocabulary. The therapist's job is to help a client 'deconstruct' their feelings (and those of others in their life), making sense of the social and moral rules/conventions involved.

Alistair, a 36-year-old white man from Scotland, told Tom, his therapist, that he became inexplicably angry in certain situations. He was always sorry afterwards. The most recent time, he said was when he had smashed his fist into the wall whilst doing some DIY. 'A red mist came down; I just snapped' he said.

The 'rules' (conventions) for the correct use of an emotion, Harré and Gillett (1994: pp. 149–50) say, fall naturally into four groups:

(1) felt bodily disturbance;
(2) characteristic display (how we 'do' the emotion);
(3) the word we choose to describe the emotion;
(4) the social act (communication).

(1) Having a strong bodily reaction when we feel an emotion gives it powerful emotional force. However, things are more complex: not all bodily feelings are called an emotion: neither feeling, nor displaying, tiredness (groaning, stretching and saying 'I'm going to bed') is seen as an emotion (Harré and Gillett 1994: p. 146). Conversely, some

emotions have a very weak bodily component. Hope, says Averill (1996) seems to lack the bodily symptoms typical of emotions. Yet, 'like anger and love, it is . . . believed to alter one's thinking and behaviour, to be out of one's control, to serve as a source of energy and sustenance, and to be part of human nature' (Harré and Parrott 1996: p. 3).

Tom explored Alistair's 'felt bodily disturbance': 'What was happening to you in the moment before you saw the 'red mist'?' I felt a kind of buzzing in my head, a kind of jangly irritated feeling . . . I wanted to run away' Tom says.

(2) The 'rules' (conventions) for a display of an emotion depend on the context. When we are angry in a church service or a committee meeting, grinding our teeth may have to suffice. In other contexts the rules allow us to be more expressive. So therapists must explore the *local* rules/conventions involved.

In the home that Alistair shared with his partner Marion the 'rules' allowed him to 'display' his anger by throwing down the hammer, hitting the wall, swearing loudly and exiting the room.

(3) The choice of an emotion word is a judgement about what the feeling, disturbance or display expresses.

Alistair described what feelings his actions expressed, he said he was 'pissed off'. This choice of emotion word/phrase describes his bodily disturbance and display: frustration/anger.

(4) The emotion display (what is said or done) performs a social act.

Alistair's actions 'tell' Marion that he is not happy with the work of putting, punded the wall up the shelves.

'Anger' in our society is seen as a natural event, something that happens to us, not something that we make a choice to 'do'. This allows diminished responsibility and this idea is framed in the language we use.

Alistair had felt the 'red mist' come over him. He threw down the hammer, punched the wall and stormed out of the room swearing. He 'had to' get out. All his actions can be excused if he is seen as being 'overcome' by anger, not totally responsible for his actions.

However, 'we "do" emotions, such as anger, in recognisable "episodes" that have beginnings, middles and ends which are learned, not innate . . . differ among cultures, and fulfill the social purposes of the angry person with suspicious regularity' says Pearce (1994: p. 178).

Tom explored the episode with Alistair: as he threw down the hammer the word 'spazzer' came to mind (an insult meaning spastic).

When we are angry we need others to help us 'enact' it (whether they are present or imaginary). And these are 'initial acts in a sequence of acts . . . held together by the conventions and rules of our society' (Harré and Gillett 1994: p. 154).

Where did this insult come from? Fellow schoolboys on the football field at school yelled it at him, when he had played badly. When the 'simple' job of putting up some shelves turned into a nightmare, Alistair connected to the frustrated, inept feeling he had had as a boy.

Instead of viewing names, concepts, words and feelings as having some kind of metaphysical *essence* and searching for conceptual similarities (in this case Alistair's 'anger') Wittgenstein (1953) offers the liberating idea of *family resemblances*.

Tom noticed that Alistair had seen/felt a 'family resemblance' between being on the football field and how he felt when putting up the shelves, exemplified by the word 'spazzer'.

A family resemblance is more like a thread, made by twisting fibre on fibre. 'And the strength of the thread does not reside in the fact that some one fibre runs through its whole length, but in the overlapping of many fibres' (Wittgenstein 1953: no. 67).

Tom, the therapist, may have also had an experience of frustration and 'anger', but this does not mean that the concept 'anger' has an essence that is shared by himself and Alistair.

We can easily see what Wittgenstein meant by 'family resemblances' says Finch (1995) by looking at the famous painting of six or seven members of the same family by Hogarth (one of Wittgenstein's favourite painters); 'we do not see a common feature in the faces, but there is nevertheless a marked . . . similarity between them all' (p. 38).

Alistair may feel the same way he did when he was a boy but this is not the same 'thing'.

Sometimes a person thinks they have encountered the same 'thing' (such as 'being bullied' or 'falling in love') but when we explore each 'fibre' there are often as many differences as there are similarities between the one event and the other.

Alistair now recalled the way that his father valued prowess in sports. As a boy he wanted to live up to these expectations, but he always failed.

Therapists ask questions that help identify who else is involved in the communication (present or imaginary), and similarities and differences between that episode and previous ones.

After the match his father would often make a disparaging remark. As a rather bookish boy there seemed to be no way that Alistair could please him. This was very different from the current episode of putting up shelves although it felt the same.

What we tend to forget is the enormous amount of 'stage-setting' that occurs in everyday life: we are born into a pre-existing culture with its rules and conventions for talking and acting. Whenever we speak we are responding to an enormously rich set of stories says Pearce (1994: p. 250). Every utterance contains traces of meaning from other utterances spoken in other social contexts, and is 'a response to a preceding utterance ... (it) refutes, affirms, supplements, and relies upon the others' (Bakhtin 1986: p. 91). And all this is usually invisible to us because we take it so much for granted. When someone says that they 'had to' behave as they did, this is a very good indication that they are following or 'obeying' a particular 'rule'.

Alistair was guided by rules/conventions (from his father and familiar in the Scottish working-class culture where he grew up) that a man must be sporty and practical.

We make sense of the emotions the person experiences by exploring their local conventions (the 'rules'), values and moral orders (in family, community and culture).

These 'rules' also allowed Alistair to express his frustration in a specific way. Asking what certain people would say about this helps identify his local conventions and moral orders.

In Western individualist societies, Averill (1982) says, the usual function of anger is seen as readjusting the terms of social relationship.

By expressing his feelings in a particular way Alistair showed Marion how he was feeling: he had wanted to make her proud of his abilities (as he had wanted to please his father) but feeling frustrated and inept with his lack of manual dexterity had reminded him of earlier lacks. Alistair's display of anger could be seen as a plea for sympathy from Marion (or maybe he was communicating something similar to his father, although he is not present?).

The meaning and expression of the emotion of 'anger' has altered over the past three centuries say Stearns and Stearns (1988 in Harré and Parrott 1996). In seventeenth-century England and Massachusetts bodily sensations and private feelings were considered irrelevant in the conception of anger. The *display* of anger was purely an expression of judgement of what someone else had done: expressing outrage and engaging in reprimand.

From another direction altogether, and counterintuitively, Laird and Apostoleris (1996 in Harré and Parrott 1996) describe some of the 'literally hundreds' of studies that show that when people are induced to act *as if* they felt something, they do, indeed, feel it (pp. 285–301). In a fascinating study Strack et al. (1988 in Harré and Parrott 1996) induced people to adopt facial expressions by asking them to hold a pen in their mouth, either in a way that produced something like a smile or an expression more like disgust. Participants reported feelings that corresponded to the induced emotion. Zajonc et al. (1989) 'asked participants to produce vowel sounds (including the 'ee' of cheese) and observed matching changes in their feelings. Feelings of confidence and pride are affected by posture say Flack et al. (1996 in Harré and Parrott 1996). If people act in a particular way, they will *feel* the corresponding emotion (pp. 288–9).

The social constructed self

'Beliefs in the individual mind ... form the cornerstone of ... the Western tradition' Gergen (1999) says, and 'To raise serious questions about the self is to send shock waves into every corner of cultural life' (p. 13). Social constructionism challenges the Western idea of an individual self that resides inside us. Instead, our selves, our identities, are created within specific historical and cultural discourse-communities.

Kate, a 23-year-old white British woman, went to see a therapist saying that she was 'not herself'. She used to be sociable, energetic and hardworking. Now she wanted to be alone, did not feel like going out, felt tired and sometimes felt tearful. 'I'm not me' she said.

The way we describe the self is a 'modern conception . . . "invented" in the 18th century' writes Pearce (1994: p. 256). 'Our "selves" are "given" to us by our society . . . we are expected to act within a cluster of rights and responsibilities deriving from our parents' position within the economic structure, the community in which we live' (p. 250). Our gender, colour, place of birth, ethnicity, physical abilities and so on, are all created within patterns of conversations, which confer identity on us. These social processes are so powerful that they are usually invisible.

Kate said that she had had a car accident a few months ago but this did not explain her personality changes: 'I should be over it by now.'

Pearce (1994) says that this is 'a far more complicated and fateful process than it seems . . . Patterns of conversations with one's parents, brothers, sisters, teachers and classmates and government officials *produce* the "self" that we know ourselves to be' (pp. 250–1).

Kate's family and social group stories involved everybody working very hard; until the accident Kate had had two jobs including helping in the family business. A 'normal' fully functioning person was busy, active and gregarious, which also fitted their middle-class values. A 'self-indulgent' ('lazy') person was 'not normal'.

Unlike the Western concept of the self as distinct from others in the community, in 'traditional non-Western cultures . . . the self is not differentiated from the nexus of social relationships in which the individual participates' (Gudykunst and Ting-Toomey 1988: p. 82). Even within Europe the term 'self' is used in many different ways: in Spanish it is difficult to express the English idea of self, whilst in French 'moi-même' does not exactly mean 'self' with the Cartesian implication of an inner entity (Muhlhausler and Harré 1991).

Kate was relieved to be allowed 'permission' and time to heal from the accident. She developed a different story: she could still be 'herself' even when she was not relentlessly productive. And it enabled her to be more empathetic with less energetic friends.

Gergen (1991) describes three different discourses or languages of the self in our culture:

- romantic;
- modernist;
- post-modern.

The romantic vocabulary talks of 'depth', 'mystery' and 'passion', originating in the 18th and 19th centuries as a protest against the reduction of human experience to rationality. 'For many, the loss of such a vocabulary would essentially be the collapse of anything meaningful in life. If love ... intrinsic worth, creative inspiration ... and passionate expression were all scratched from our vocabularies, life for many would be a pallid affair indeed' (Gergen 1991: p. 27).

Modernist languages view the self as a fixed and knowable entity: finding one's 'true self', valuing autonomy, rationality, and reliability. A healthy person aims to be 'self-directing', 'trustworthy', 'consistent', 'genuine' ... 'principled' not craven, stable not wavering (Gergen 1991: p. 44).

However, in post-modern languages huge social and intellectual changes have questioned any ability to discover a single vocabulary of the self: we 'exist in a state of continuous construction and reconstruction' (Gergen 1991: pp. 5–6). Constructionism creates a new language, says Pearce (1994), a 'bricolage', 'picking up bits and pieces of leftover language and integrating them into a new language' (p. 264) which Stout (1988: p. 75) says all creativity involves.

A sense of one's personal individuality, Harré and Gillett (1994) write, involves having 'a sense of a location in space, literally a point of view'. Studying the use of first and second-person pronouns, they say, can help us understand how the self is produced discursively, in conversation. But we must be wary of seeing English as the standard from which other languages deviate, particularly since English has a paucity of pronouns compared, for example, to Japanese. In Japan two people in a conversation can refer to 'something like 260 different social relations using pronouns and verb inflections' (pp. 105–6). This leads to a much richer idea of the 'self' from the one 'I' in our culture that stands for one's body, physical location, moral obligations, autobiography and so on.

The self, in cultures like ours, 'influenced by the Judeo-Christian moral system ... means having a sense of myself as a moral agent, located in a network of mutual obligations and commitments' (Harré and Gillett 1994: pp. 103–4). The 'sense that one is agent of one's actions and responsible to others for them, is something that we acquire through learning the language and cultural conventions' (p. 111). When we act, we often refer to some moral reason, which includes an explanation based on our identity (Cronen et al. 1979).

If I were in the pub with a group of friends I might think 'I must buy a round of drinks when it is my turn' (because 'a person like me' could not act otherwise).

Vygotsky (1986 in Shotter 1995) says that learning manual skills is just as necessary for acquiring a sense of self as the learning of verbal skills.

If, after taking people's orders, I go to the bar, order the drinks, pay for them and bring them back, I am developing my 'self' through a combination of 'moral reason', language skills and manual skills.

'Position' and one's right to speak

There are important differences between the rights (and duties) that different people have in the world, particularly their ability to enter a conversation.

Jenny, a young black social worker, may have fewer rights to give her opinion at a child protection case conference than the white male psychiatrist or white female paediatrician.

The 'position' we occupy in the world creates our sense of self and creates certain emotions.

After this had happened several times Jenny came to describe herself as a 'hard-working but unimportant' professional; she may feel undervalued and experience all the emotions attached to that.

A 'position' is a set of rights, duties, and obligations particularly with respect to what one may say in a certain context. The concept of 'positioning' was first devised by Holloway (1984) say Harré and Gillett (1994: pp. 34–5). The different positions that we occupy in society offer certain rights and duties, and can describe what is happening in certain contexts without having to refer to an individual's intrapsychic personality traits.

In mixed groups Holloway found that women say less than men: women in mixed groups are 'positioned' as having fewer rights than men to offer their views or criticise a male speaker. However, in same-sex groups women talk more than men in all-male groups do. An adult is usually positioned as having more rights to speak than a child does. In a work setting a professional is positioned as having more rights than a student. People from non-dominant racial and ethnic groups are generally permitted fewer rights than those who are from the dominant culture.

Social and economic factors

Social factors, such as our accents, access to specialist knowledge (such as medical languages) and so on can affect how others describe us and what discourses and communities we can join. Also, since problem-saturated stories are nested in social, cultural, economic and gender assumptions, systemic therapists must be thoroughly conversant with the social and historical biases inherent in certain theories. In child development certain ideas that led to social engineering practices, such as separating Maori children from their parents in order to give them a 'better future', were once seen as 'common sense' but have since been reversed and reviled.

Socio-economic imbalances and the 'crushing effects of poverty and stress' affect the ways in which people live and what opportunities they have write Dallos and Draper (2000: 94). Sapolsky (1998) says that poorer people have the most stressors and a disproportionate share of disease regardless of gender or race (p. 308). And, as we have seen, these affect a person's sense of self and their emotions. An excellent edition of the systemic journal *Human Systems* (1994) devoted entirely to poverty, shows ways in which we can confront these issues. Imelda McCarthy urges us to question the 'normative practice base' which used the male experience of the nuclear family as a principal referent (1994: 23). Reflecting on their own practice Waldegrave and Tamasese (1994: 194), from the 'Just Therapy' group in New Zealand, critique the way they had been treating 'events like unemployment, bad housing or homelessness, racist or sexist experiences ... as though they were symptoms of family dysfunction'. They then recognised that these were 'symptoms of poverty, of unjust economic planning' and so on.

It *is* possible to work both with the social effects of economic and other inequalities *and* a client's relationship says Jones (1994: 169–83). This is not a case of *either* working with personal and interactional issues *or* doing something at a broader cultural and political level, but more a truly social constructionist stance of both/and: our therapeutic conversations *are* political ones.

Feelings and emotions

- are culturally and historically specific;
- relate to specific gender, class, family, religious and personal identity stories;
- are co-constructed through communication processes and language (verbal and non-verbal);
- are social 'roles' that we enact in brief 'episodes' within specific contexts;
- are statements: communications to specific people (whether present or absent);
- usually involve a bodily feeling, a moral 'judgement', a description and a communication;
- are connected to our position in the world;
- can be induced by a particular facial expression or body posture.

The self is

- a social, cultural and historical construction;
- co-constructed within ongoing conversations;
- not necessarily a separate individual (this is a Western construction);
- co-constructed within cultural, economic (and other) contexts;
- developed through both manual and verbal skills;
- co-constructed through particular pronoun use.

Social and economic factors and our position in society

- grant certain people rights (to speak, act and so on);
- allow, or deny, access to discourses and communities;
- affect the way others 'hear', 'see' and describe us;
- powerfully affect a person's physiological health and well being.

4
THE IMPORTANCE OF CONTEXT

Do not think that an action or a word is its own sufficient definition. I believe that an action or the label put on an experience must always be seen . . . in context
                                                                  Bateson (1972)

What defines us as systemic is our interest in context and the way that meaning is socially constructed, contextually defined and is therefore capable of being changed
                                                                  Jones and Asen (2000)

Words do not have any inherent meaning, they only make sense when we know the context in which they are used
                                                                  Wittgenstein (1953)

Therapists who use systemic social constructionist practices place *context* at the heart of our approach. There are, however, many ways in which context informs our work. One way is that in every context there is potential for numerous meanings if we are willing to see them.

A television advertisement some years ago showed a young punk running full tilt along the pavement and pushing past idling shoppers. He runs towards an older woman with a handbag. She looks round, startled as he stretches his arm out towards her. We assume that he is about to mug her. Then the camera pulls back and we see him pushing her out of the way of a falling piece of debris.

This clever piece of filming (advertising *The Guardian* newspaper) showed that new information can shift the context and the meaning of the action; in this case the young man went from 'villain' to 'quick-thinking hero' in one move. By seeing his action in a different context unnoticed aspects become visible and the whole meaning of the interaction is irrevocably altered. Shotter writes 'By shifting one's stance and position in relation to one's surroundings, yet further unnoticed aspects become visible' (1997: 16).

In this approach we work with the idea that there are no universal meanings in our social worlds; this helps us become curious about our clients' *unique, local* and *specific* contexts and stories, rather than searching for pre-existing theories into which to fit them. We appreciate clients' *particular stories* about identity, family, culture, ethnicity, colour, race, religion, gender, class and age amongst many others. We also recognise the impact of *our contexts* on clients and ourselves. The language we use, our style, manner, tone, gestures, personal and professional stories and our relationships within the setting in which we work will affect therapeutic conversations. Recognising all this enriches our practice and makes it more effective.

The *OED*'s definition of 'context' is, 'the parts that immediately precede or follow a word or passage and clarify its meaning'. However, using *context* simply as a noun, as in asking 'what is the context?' that is, the social setting of a word or action, is a trap, since this creates an assumption that context exists in the world as a *thing*. But like any term, the meaning comes from how we use it in our communications with others.

If we return to the original Latin/Middle English definition we see context as a *process* of making connections and co-creating meanings: '*contextus*... means "woven/sewn together or connected... the connexion or coherence between the parts of discourse... the weaving together of words"' (*OED* 19: 820/1). How does this weaving work in the way that we do therapeutic work?

The meaning of a word or an action depends on the context in which it takes place

Cronen and Pearce's (1991/92) communication model CMM (Co-ordinated Management of Meaning) elegantly demonstrates how we weave (socially construct) meanings in our conversations with each other. This model warrants a more thorough discussion to appreciate its complexity, however, the important principle is that particular stories and actions affect a context and the context in turn affects those stories and actions.

When I am with particular friends in the context of a relaxed evening I connect to the self-identity story that I am witty, and may act in a silly, humorous way. But in the context of a committee meeting in which my ideas appear to be undervalued I connect to a very different story. This will affect how I talk, act and feel.

Drawing on Wittgenstein's later work, Pearce (1994) says that the language we use and other actions are influenced by what we perceive as the context in which we act (p. 114). It is not so much that I am 'a witty person' in the first context or I am 'an inarticulate person' in the second, it is that each context connects me to certain stories and voices. Using these ideas enables us to help clients make sense of how influential stories affect their responses in a particular context. Certain stories may arise in the context of the person's relationship with the therapist, and/or their family, peer group, and/or the culture in which they live, and so on.

Jenny, a white British woman, could not understand why she had acted 'violently and out of character' when she and her husband Ron were at a party. Although she had been having a good time with friends, she suddenly threw a glass of wine at him, and burst into tears. She had noticed that her husband had been dancing with another, much younger woman.

The therapist may think 'Ah-ha, Jenny was simply jealous of the attention her husband was paying to the other woman; this *explains* her behaviour.'

'Were you jealous of that woman?' the therapist asks. 'Um, maybe' Jenny says doubtfully, 'but not all that jealous'. She says that they have always behaved in a flirtatious way with friends at parties. And the woman was a friend whose boyfriend also accepted this.

So the therapist's original 'explanation' does not quite fit. When we attempt to fit the client's story into pre-existing ideas then this tends to curtail the potentially numerous contexts and descriptions to which the client *could* be connecting.

'What else came to mind in the moment that you threw the wine?' the therapist asks. Jenny now wonders if her impending 40th birthday was a relevant factor.

Maybe age is an important context: 40 could be seen as a 'tricky' age, the other woman was younger than Jenny and youth and attractiveness are linked in our culture.

The therapist explores what nearing 40 means to Jenny. This does not yield anything relevant. However, after some questioning she makes a connection with a powerful family story: when her mother was about 40 and she was 16, her father had left them and 'ruined their life' (financial hardship and her mother's hurt and anger affected Jenny's relationship with both her parents for some years).

Again, the therapist could believe that this 'explains' her behaviour: in the context of being a wife nearing her 40th birthday, disaster looms. The therapist could connect to a theory of abandonment, loss and grief and anger towards her father.

Yet, soon after her parents' split and the initial distress Jenny says that her mother was relieved as she and her husband were not well suited. Jenny forgave her father for leaving them. Both parents had subsequently remarried happily.

So again, the idea that she was identifying with the context of her mother's distress and anger did not quite fit.

'What's Ron's idea?' the therapist asks. Jenny says that he has always made it clear that marriage is for life. He was puzzled about Jenny's actions; in the context of a stable marriage he saw dancing with another woman as 'harmless fun'.

When a story does not fit it is useful to explore other contexts to which the client could be connecting. 'We are never in one conversation at a time' says Pearce (1994). 'Each act we perform is at the nexus of many conversations, each with its own logic of meaning and action' (p. 35).

The therapist now explores who else is significant in Jenny's life. She immediately talks about their 14-year-old daughter Jade, who has learning difficulties, which make both parents want to protect her.

The therapist wondered whether this context is important. Did she want to protect her vulnerable daughter from a fate similar to her own ('abandoned', albeit temporarily, by her father at 14)?

The therapist carefully explored this context. 'What would happen to their daughter should the worst happen and Jenny and Ron's marriage breaks up?' Jenny feels sure that neither of them would want to separate. How is she so sure? Ron needs a lot of reassurance from her. She has always provided that. As she talks she now remembers that her aunt (her mother's sister) had believed that Jenny's mother had not shown her husband that she had loved him – and had therefore 'lost' him. It was her aunt's words 'show him that you care' that had come to mind during that party.

She had connected to that story and this had 'made her' act in the dramatic way she did. But there was yet another important context: that of her relationship with Ron.

Exploring the 'logic' of crying, Jenny realised that she needed to communicate to her husband that she did not want to hurt and upset him.

Here we can see how various contexts had been woven together into one piece of action. This is very different from using a particular piece of theory, like saying *she was afraid of being abandoned by her husband (as her mother had been, at a similar age)*, and 'placing it on' the client's story.

Working with context can be difficult for therapists who prefer the safety of fitting clients into theories, descriptions and typologies, but when we see the effects on clients' lives this is exciting and wonderfully liberating.

Pearce's (1994) 'atomic' model is a heuristic device that neatly demonstrates this. It provides one way to help us answer the question 'what is going on here?' (p. 34) (see Figure 1). This model does not show the many contexts to which Ron (or anybody else) was connecting. It is a 'snapshot', a moment in time from Jenny's perspective only, and shows the many contexts and conversations to which Jenny was connecting in that moment.

'Hearing' her aunt's voice helped Jenny to understand her actions; she was able to have a different conversation with Ron.

When we are in one context we can connect to a personal identity story, gender, family, ethnic, colour, class, religion, political, economic, sexual story and so on.

Even when we are alone, we may connect to powerful stories and strong voices depending on what context we think we are in.

Maria, a 16-year-old Turkish Cypriot woman, was referred to therapy as she was cutting herself. Maria could not talk openly; however, she eventually said that when she was alone she constantly called herself insulting names; cutting herself was 'a relief'. The therapist patiently explored the meaning of the words and the contexts in which she harmed herself. Maria said she was 'very bad' because she had disobeyed her mother by buying a mobile phone in order to ring her boyfriend. Maria had been forbidden

SYSTEMIC THERAPY WITH INDIVIDUALS

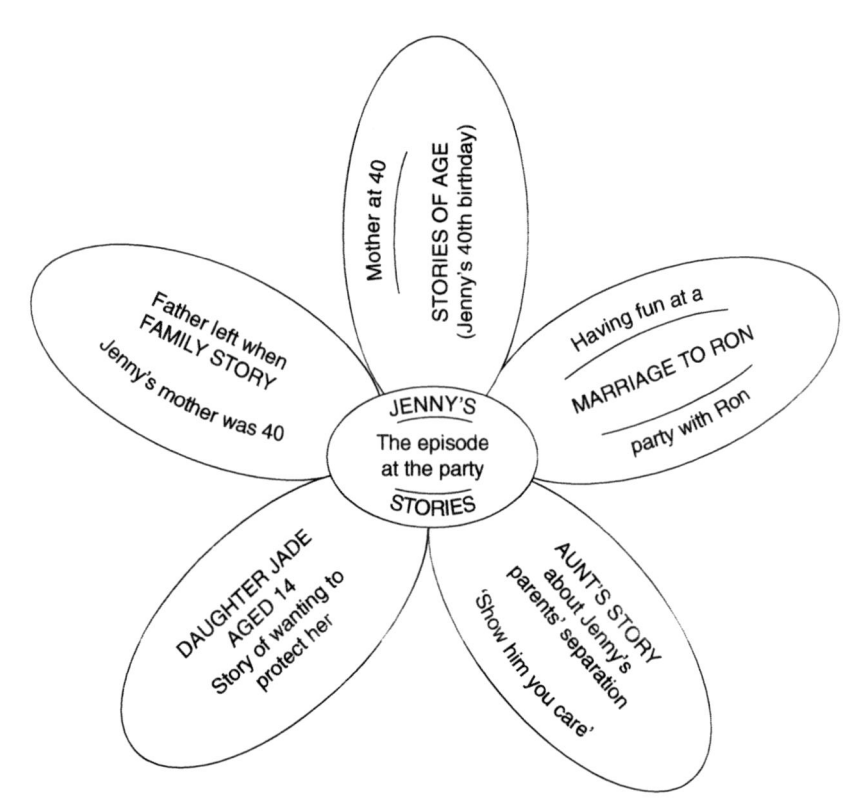

Figure 1 Pearce's 'atomic' model

Petals of the flower diagram:
- STORIES OF AGE (Jenny's 40th birthday) — Mother at 40
- MARRIAGE TO RON — Having fun at a party with Ron
- AUNT'S STORY about Jenny's parents' separation — 'Show him you care'
- DAUGHTER JADE AGED 14 — Story of wanting to protect her
- FAMILY STORY — Father left when Jenny's mother was 40

Centre: JENNY'S STORIES — The episode at the party

to have a boyfriend. Her mother had found the phone and had read the text messages Maria had sent and received. Her mother had screamed abuse at her, calling her a 'tart' and a 'whore'. The words were accompanied by slaps. Although Maria was shocked at the force of her mother's anger she was not surprised and was in fact deeply ashamed of herself.

The therapist explored the family and cultural contexts in which these events had happened.

Maria was brought up by strict Turkish Cypriot parents who had come to the more 'permissive' British culture before her birth. Maria was torn between wanting to be a 'good' daughter and doing things that were considered normal in her peer-group.

One could say that Maria was 'caught' between two competing contexts, and/or that she felt loyal to *both* contexts.

Maria says that her father had often called her 'bad names' when she was growing up; now she has learned to use even more graphically abusive words about herself whenever she does something 'wrong'.

It takes time to disentangle interwoven contexts. What made Maria's father so harsh? Here, a family story told within the context of culture and religion helped make sense of Maria's parents' attitudes and her behaviour.

Maria's parents were determined to preserve their deep religious faith. In the context of being 'good Catholics' they were afraid that the 'irreligious' British culture would corrupt their daughter. But it was a particular family story that was informing them. Maria's father had come from a 'better' family than her mother and his parents were against the marriage. The family story became 'No good will come of this marriage.' So, when Maria's aunt (her mother's sister) had a baby out of wedlock when she was 18, this had 'proved' his family right. In the context of the rifts created between the two families, Maria's parents worked even harder to ensure that Maria did not follow her aunt's suit. This made them highly vigilant about Maria's behaviour.

By appreciating the powerful influences of specific voices and stories that can affect a person's 'self stories', the therapist can offer some different ways of making sense of their current feelings and actions.

In the context of trying very hard to be 'good' parents, their harsh words made sense. Her mother's extreme distress when she discovered the mobile phone and the existence of a forbidden boyfriend could be seen as a way of 'protecting' her from her aunt's fate. When Maria recognised this, her self-hatred lessened. Eventually she found less need to berate herself and to self-harm.

Clarifying the context for therapeutic work

Bateson (1972) noted three significant contexts that operate within every conversation:

- the context of time;
- the context of the definition of relationship;
- the context of place.

When we meet a client we set aside a specific period of *time* as a boundary which 'sets the context' for a special kind of conversation. We normally meet in a particular *place*, although there are many variations on the conventional room with two chairs. Because meanings are co-created within the context of relationships, we define *the relationship* as being of a particular kind. However, it is important to be willing to discuss and clarify assumptions and expectations about the meaning that a client puts on a therapeutic conversation. This demonstrates that we value the client as the 'expert in their life'.

Since relationships are made in conversations and conversations are made by the imperfect way in which we coordinate meanings, all relationships are open-ended and mutable. If we work within a particular agency, the relationship the client has with this is also crucial.

A specific place can connect us to particular feelings, thoughts and actions. We call this 'context-dependent learning'.

Benjamin, an African-Caribbean man of 36, came to see me after he had taken an overdose. At the end of the first session he made it clear that he wanted to see me the following week and I respected this. We met every week and I began to notice that he was unable to respond to my opening questions such as 'what are your hopes for today's conversation?' that were intended to set the context and provide a focus for the session. Each week he had no idea about what he wanted; it became a form of humour between us. Another thing that puzzled me was that, despite the many hopeful changes in his life, he invariably opened the conversation by relating something bad that he had said or done. This did not fit with what was actually going on (his 'stories lived') so I asked him to help me to understand the discrepancy. He then 'confessed' that he had seen a psychiatrist for several months the previous year. The psychiatrist expected him to go every week and to talk about ways in which he could do better. Or this is how Benjamin had experienced their conversations.

The context of place, talking to a professional, was informing him about another therapeutic context.

Realising this, Benjamin began to talk about the many ways in which he was doing well.

Inviting the client to join a particular context

What we say when we first meet a client and at all subsequent meetings invites the client into a particular kind of context, or conversation, in Wittgenstein's (1953) term a 'language game'. The meaning of a word or action depends on the context or 'language game' in which it takes place (talking *is* action). Therefore it is important to think about what context we are setting with a client when we first meet them. A therapeutic conversation is special time. So, asking 'How would you like to use the time we have together today?' signals this to the client. Asking 'What would you like to focus on?' invites the client to make decisions about the *focus* of the session. And by asking 'What would you like to work on today?' we set the context for *work*.

If, however, the therapist says 'what seems to be the problem?' a context of 'problem-seeking' is co-created. If we ask 'How can I help you?' this creates the context of a helper and a person who is to be helped. If we sit silently and wait for the client to talk he or she may not know how to respond, or may view this as an invitation into free-association. When we meet the person we ask ourselves what 'language game' are we inviting the client to join; is this one of 'therapist knows best' or one of negotiation and co-creation?

When systemic therapists ask questions we set a context of *learning* about clients' specific contexts. A question like 'What are you hoping for from this conversation?' (and/or therapy?) introduces hope at an early stage, helps the client to clarify their expectations and helps them decide what they want from therapy.

Sandra, a 42-year-old Greek woman said that these questions 'cracked open a door to the future' which she had never before dared to explore.

Context markers

If someone says 'I love you' in an angry or sarcastic tone there is a confusion of contexts, which Bateson said could create a 'double bind', since one would not know whether to believe in the verbal or the non-verbal message or which was the main context.

Therefore we use *context markers* to clarify the context and enable ourselves to shift from one context to another.

It is raining. The therapist invites Rose, a 52-year-old Portuguese woman, to take off her coat and hang it up. 'Ghastly weather' she says and Rose agrees. This can be seen as a context of 'welcoming'. Both sit down and the therapist asks Rose what she would like to work on today. This opening question signals that they have moved to the context of talking.

Bateson (1972) originally noticed that monkeys who were nipping each other playfully used *context markers* to indicate that they were in the context of 'play' rather than a context of 'combat'. They would signal this by nipping and nuzzling interchangeably. He says that these signs or signals showed that they had the ability to meta-communicate (to communicate about the whole communication) (p. 179).

Angelina, a 45-year-old Irish woman, came to see me at the suggestion of her GP. I noticed that she constantly frowned and screwed up her face as if in pain. Indeed she was in considerable physical pain she said and had asked to be referred to a pain management clinic, but this had not happened. Apart from the effect of the pain, her life was good. Unfortunately her grimaces gave her the appearance of someone who was not very bright, whereas she was actually a bright professional woman. When I tentatively asked whether her facial expressions were a way to 'tell' people about the pain she was astounded that this was what she had been communicating and I referred to the way I had been speaking more slowly than usual. She found my meta-communication extremely useful. We then had a more flowing conversation and she vowed not to make these facial expressions, unless she was in an appropriate context.

Acting out of and into contexts

We simultaneously act 'out of' numerous contexts and 'into' other contexts that we imagine, perceive or invent, and together we constantly co-create new meanings (Pearce 1994: p. 209).

When a client comes to therapy they 'act out of' the numerous stories about themselves arising from their unique position in life, their gender, age, colour, ethnicity and so on. They will also have ideas about what constitutes a therapeutic conversation and what it can do for them, based on societal stories or (as we have seen) their own previous experience. They will 'act into' the context of therapy based on the context we have set through our publicity material, what others say about us, our geographical and physical environment as well as our own style and manner.

Contexts out of which clients are acting

Every client will come with unique stories drawn from their position in their family and community, their personal identity stories, political affiliations, their age and gender, their class, culture, specific religious and ethical values. They will have unique skin colour, body size and so on. They will be embodied, normally within a male or female body, although this in itself is an assumption, as about one in a thousand will be born intersexed (Geertz 1983: pp. 80–1). There will be particular physiological advantages and disadvantages to their embodiment. All these contexts inform clients' stories. Our job is to be curious about them.

Contexts out of which therapists are acting

Therapists' professional and personal contexts have the potential for enormous power in the conversation.

Joan, a 34-year-old white British woman, told her therapist that she had recently been divorced. The therapist inevitably connected to many societal, cultural, religious and personal stories about divorce, such as the idea that Joan's marriage had 'failed', that she might feel hurt and angry or that as a woman she could be disadvantaged financially.

When we work with clients we draw from a wealth of personal and professional stories. But they may not be relevant to this particular client.

The therapist asked Joan about the specific context of her divorce, and she said that whilst she does feel lonely at times, she is enjoying the physical space and that divorce has meant financial independence.

As with clients, our personal stories derived from numerous contexts affect how we think, feel, talk and act. In addition we will also have political ideas and stories from our professional training about best practice, preferred ways of working, ideas about what is 'normal' and 'abnormal', experiences of working with particular kinds of issues and so on.

If I have been able to do successful therapeutic work with young women who have starved themselves I will be more optimistic than someone who has not had these experiences.

The therapeutic setting: the context into which clients are acting

When a person comes for help the context into which they believe they are acting, their view of us and the contexts in which we work are extremely important in shaping their expectations of therapy. Also, what other people say about us can also affect what clients think about us. Particular stories that clients and other professionals tell about our service or agency will affect our conversations, and co-create the stories that people tell about therapy in general. So the way we communicate both verbally and in writing can enhance or damage these relationships.

I once spoiled the easy access I had with a patient who was staying in a psychiatric hostel by a chance remark about their rather strict rules, which the warden overheard on a telephone extension.

Clients may connect with specific stories; they may have heard that 'this place helps people sort out their benefits, but you have to tell them your life story first.' Or 'my friend felt better after she talked to someone here.' Some people may work in contexts that are less conventional than a room in a building.

A colleague lives and works in a small religious community and she goes out on the streets to meet sex workers in their own contexts. Because of the respectful and humorous way in which the Sisters work, one vulnerable young woman said 'I don't believe in all that God rubbish but I'd rather trust you than anybody.'

We can become so accustomed to the geographical area, the building, the name of our place of work and our own job title that very often we forget the impact of this on those who come to talk to us.

A client once said that the title on my door 'Head of the Counselling Service' made him feel nervous. He wondered whether I would be in regular conversations with the head of his department.

Clients may make assumptions about conversations that are taking place between the professionals involved, unless we explore the relationships between all of us and clarify the confidentiality issues.

When we have worked in a system for some time we may take the referral system for granted, rather than exploring the meanings of that process with the person who comes to talk with us. But if we are curious about the unique pathway that the client took to reach us this will give us useful information about their network of relationships.

Ben, a 16-year-old white British boy, whose family had been involved with Social Services for many years, had refused to talk to all professionals, but when his mates said that the people at a local voluntary project were 'all right', he talked to the therapist there.

If a therapist works within a context such as a GP surgery, hospital, or community mental health service, clients may assume that the therapist will share the same 'language games' of health and illness, diagnosis, treatment and medication.

When I worked as a hospital psychiatric social worker, Geraldine, a 62-year-old Italian woman with complex family issues who had been 'in the psychiatric system' for over 25 years, was referred to me for therapy by her new consultant psychiatrist. My conversations with Geraldine were frustrating and repetitive until I explored the processes of the referral and discovered that she had a strong story that because she regularly saw a psychiatrist and took medication she 'must be mad', there was something wrong with her brain and she was incurable. All our conversations about her current, future and past relationships made no sense to her because every time she saw the psychiatrist her 'mad' story was reconfirmed. Although the consultant affirmed that talking could be helpful, the very fact that she had regular appointments with him and received medication continually reconnected her to the 'madness is untreatable' story. I would like to report that we were able to destabilise this powerful story, but the context of 'merely talking' with a lowly social worker was always superseded by the context of place (Psychiatric Out-Patients) and the context of relationship (a male high-status consultant psychiatrist).

Setting the context for a therapeutic conversation

By 'setting the context' we mean 'locating' or situating, not 'setting' as in aspic or stone. Even before any therapist speaks to, or meets, a client, the design and language of any publicity material set a particular context for potential clients.

Talking with clients for many years can blind us to the meaning of a first meeting for a client, so being willing to notice the 'taken-for-granted' by taking the client's reactions seriously is another way in which we show respect. Everything, from the geographical environment, the type of organisation in which we work (if we do), to the building and the room creates meaning for clients. Going to talk to somebody in Social Services has a different meaning from going to a private house. The area and the building itself will all create important communications for clients who go to see a private therapist, as well as the décor and the objects in the room. Our clothes, manner, tone of voice and accent will all help to create a particular kind of context. My preference is for a comfortable setting and a warm, welcoming yet professional approach and manner. However, we can never know what meaning the client will take from any of these.

Julia, a white British woman in her early 30s, said that a flower painting in the waiting area was 'middle-class' and off-putting, whilst my intention was to create a beautiful calming atmosphere.

All these aspects create an invitation to join a particular kind of narrative into which the client will act. There can be any number of expectations, which are useful to clarify at the outset. For example we do not know what prior experiences they have heard about therapeutic conversations.

However, Julia appreciated my interactive style as she said that the many counsellors/therapists she had tried had allowed her to sit in silence for much of the session, which had been unproductive.

We also get important information when we check out why and for what reasons the client has decided to come to talk to us. We may find that another professional, or a partner, a family member or friend has made the suggestion, which will help us to map the network of their relationships. The early Milan team's paper 'The problem of the referring person' shows how other people's concern can create 'a person with a problem' (Selvini et al. 1980).

When a therapist working in a GP surgery asked Carla, a 55-year-old African woman, what made her decide to make an appointment she was puzzled: she had simply followed her GP's advice after she had cried in the surgery.

Sharon, a white British woman in her late 20s who was doing a degree in Psychology and Counselling, went to see one of the therapists at the

University Counselling Service but could not articulate her needs or wishes despite the therapist's patience and inventiveness. Exploring how she had got the idea to come to talk, Sharon said that a tutor had urged everyone to 'work on their personal issues' if they were to be of any use to others. She had followed this suggestion but had little idea what she wanted to talk about.

Transparency

Being transparent means being open and clear with clients about our ways of working. Systemic therapists prefer to involve clients in collaborative conversations about frequency of meetings, focus for the work and so on. The position we take is that the therapist is the participant-manager of the conversation and the client is the expert in their life (Anderson and Goolishian 1988, 1992). Whilst *we* can help in the process *they* will make ultimate decisions about how to live their lives.

It is important to be transparent about one's qualifications, confidentiality policies and so on. Those who work in specific contexts will have other policies to which they must adhere. This may entail offering a certain number of sessions or working within a geographical location or with a certain client group. Having clearly written publicity information is invaluable, but it helps to clarify the meaning verbally with each client.

In the Counselling Service at Roehampton University where I work transparency means offering clients access to their notes; we have developed a way of involving clients in the co-creation of their notes in the first session, which they can later modify (Hedges 2000) (see Appendix 2 to this volume).

Negotiating the fee

Discussing the fee can bring private therapists out in a cold sweat. It is useful to decide whether to have a sliding scale or to simply have a standard fee and negotiate with each client. Negotiation is a central part of systemic approaches so therapists must be prepared to negotiate about money. It is also important to clarify whether the client is expected to pay for the session if they cancel it less than 24 hours in advance and so on. Inviting a partner or family member may involve a different fee, particularly if another therapist is involved.

Making an appointment with a client on the telephone

The telephone is often the first contact that a client makes with a therapist or agency, and this first impression is crucial. Managing this process requires enormous, much-undervalued skill, whether this is done by a receptionist or by the therapist. The tone, manner, pace and the actual words used will 'set the context' for how the potential client or referrer describes the therapeutic setting. If a non-therapist answers the telephone, a professional, warm, courteous, gentle yet *brief,* response will define the relationship clearly as that of 'receptionist' and the context as 'making an appointment', rather than responding to distress or giving information about the process.

I was given a useful piece of advice about making appointments on the telephone when I worked in a complementary health centre. Instead of saying 'I can't offer you an appointment until . . .' a better way is to say 'I am able to offer you an appointment on . . . at . . .'.

If we have to telephone a new client in response to their inquiry it is important to be sensitive. Mobile phones can be extremely convenient in one way but pose other problems, since the person may not be in a convenient or confidential place where they can talk. It is therefore best to:

- choose an appropriate time to call;
- identify the name of the person who answers;
- explain who you are;
- check out if it is a convenient time;
- not declare one's profession (or agency), if another person answers the telephone;
- use the title appropriate to the context: in some agencies one may be called a 'counsellor' or have some other title.

Negotiating a contract

In some agency contexts there are contractual issues that must be addressed at the outset. These can include:

- the length of the sessions;
- whether there is to be a different length of time for the first meeting from subsequent ones;

- the frequency of meetings;
- how frequency is agreed;
- whether the client is likely to be referred on to another therapist (or agency) after the first meeting;
- the arrangements for making and cancelling appointments;
- the number of sessions that can be offered;
- the length of time that a client can continue to have therapy;
- arrangements for holidays;
- fees (if relevant);
- discussion of other therapies as well as talking;
- how far clients can negotiate any of the above.

It is also important to discuss the issue of confidentiality, particularly if another professional has referred the client. Therapists can make the assumption that they will not discuss the client with other professionals, but may need to spell this out and outline briefly the circumstances in which confidentiality could be broken, such as if the client becomes a danger to him or herself or another. Having printed information also clarifies the context.

If workers are in multiple roles and contexts, it is crucial to discuss the different rights and responsibilities involved within each context. This is also useful when there is a mixture of family therapy, group and individual work, where the client may fear that information disclosed in the individual session could be inadvertently 'leaked' in other contexts.

Workers who do a mixture of formal and informal, practical and therapeutic work will find it helpful to clarify the context of a particular conversation. Lang et al.'s (1990) concept of 'domains' is useful: in the 'domain of productivity' one could be organising something practical; in the 'domain of explanation' one is doing therapeutic talking work. Simply by moving from an easy chair to a desk will signal that one is moving from one context to another, but doing this verbally also helps.

Multiple contexts

In some settings we may have relationships with other workers that involve several different roles or positions, for example we may work with someone who is our manager in one context, but a colleague in a systemic team seeing a family in another context. A supervisor may also become a friend, or a friend may become a supervisor. These multiple-contextual relationships create many opportunities for misunderstandings if we do not clarify the rights, responsibilities, contractual implications and the expectations of each context. Yet they also afford many opportunities for creative work. It is useful to recall Bateson's three context markers: time, place and relationship. So, for each context one could meet in a different place, clarify the time that has been set aside for that specific task and define the relationship by giving it a title.

Context

- Every client comes from, *'acts out of'*, a *unique* set of contexts.
- When we talk with a client we are *'acting into'* their contexts.
- Every therapist comes from, *'acts out of'*, a *unique* set of contexts.
- When a client comes to talk they are *acting into* our contexts.
- Thus we *co-create* a new unique context with the client.
- When a client describes thoughts, feelings and actions in their lives all these have taken place within *the context of particular relationships*.
- The language we use fits into a particular context, that is, a statement, question, demand and so on. (Wittgenstein (1953) called these 'language games'.)
- Words do not have an intrinsic meaning, but *a use only within a context* – they are best seen as tools or instruments for use in the making of meanings.
- We use a sign or signal as a *context marker*, to indicate a new context.
- Signalling a new context requires the ability to *communicate about the communication*: to meta-communicate.
- All actions are communications and verbal (and non-verbal) language *is* action.
- Being clear about the context helps to prevent misunderstandings.

Therapists working with context will

- explore the therapist–client context with clients;
- be transparent about the impact of our contexts/organisations on the client;
- explore clients' expectations of therapy;
- clarify the relevant policies of our agency with the client;
- explore the client's specific *local* contexts (relationships and stories);
- involve clients in continuing conversations about the effects of all relevant contexts on them (including political, economic, cultural contexts and so on);
- explore ways in which our personal contexts (self-identity, family, culture and so on) and professional contexts (agencies, political stories and so on) affect our conversations with clients.

5
FROM NEUTRALITY AND CURIOSITY TO SELF–OTHER-REFLEXIVITY

It is impossible to be curious when we are 'true believers'
                                                    Cecchin (1992)

Every sacred cow in the field is sacred for only a moment
                                       Keeney in Cecchin et al. (1992)

The Milan team's innovative trio of concepts 'hypothesising, circularity and neutrality' are interrelated; when we refer to one, we inevitably call up the other two (Selvini et al. 1980). Firstly, I discuss the usefulness of 'neutrality' then the various transmutations: 'curiosity', 'irreverence' and 'self-reflexivity'. I explore them in the chronological order that they evolved, but these are false distinctions, since they overlap in many ways.

It is useful to bear in mind that: (1) no concept is universally beneficial; it is the context that determines its usefulness; (2) any concept we use guides the moral position we take with our clients. Therefore, we must always ask ourselves what the consequences are of using any concept.

We recognise, Cecchin (1987: 405) writes, that 'all behaviour, including language, is politically laden.' '... "neutrality" was originally used to express the idea of actively avoiding the acceptance of any one position as more correct than another' (Cecchin 1987: 405–6).

Neutrality

Jonti, a 45-year-old Nigerian woman, came to therapy to explore why she was feeling so anxious and sad. She had recently come to England with her two teenage daughters to help them get a better education whilst she pursued her dream of becoming a teacher. I explored in detail her past frus-

trations with her 'short-tempered', 'mean' husband, her current dilemmas with accommodation, and her hopes to become a professional.

'If a therapist had been successful in being neutral, by the end of the session the family would not know whether anybody's view or position was favoured' (Boscolo et al. 1987: p. 97).

Jonti missed her friends back home and felt dislocated in London but she planned to settle here and divorce her husband, who was still in Nigeria. She described him as, 'a workaholic' and 'not a proper husband or father'. After 18 years she had had enough. I connected strongly to her compelling story.

'We as therapists are always taking positions . . . therapist and client . . . are always acting on and reflecting their ideologies, their values and their views. Neutrality is not not having a position but, rather, always evolving new interpretative positions' write Anderson and Goolishian (1988: 385).

I felt empathetic towards Jonti and her story, but recognised that there may also be other ways of telling it; for example, I wondered what the other people in her life might say.

'Neutrality' was originally the Milan team's basic stance: a way of seeing everybody (in 'the system') as *doing the best they can, given all the circumstances.* It is inextricably linked with the *positive (or logical) connotation* (see Chapter 2). Although there are major problems with 'neutrality', it is still useful, writes Jones (1993) if only to demonstrate what the Milan team was rebelling against. The Milan team (Selvini et al. 1980) developed the concept of neutrality to prevent them siding with, or blaming anyone (in the family) *or their behaviour.* The Milan team attempted to be neutral towards everybody's point of view *including their own.* And they strove to maintain neutrality towards outcomes. This was 'an improvement on the crassly punitive, judgmental and pathologizing behaviour, which flows easily from a first-order cybernetic perspective' says Jones (1993: pp. 145–6). Therapists taking a 'first-order cybernetic' perspective focus *primarily* on the client's stories making the assumption that the therapist can be an objective observer.

One critique of neutrality was that 'for many therapists neutrality has been regarded as the cultivation of a position of non-involvement, of not having strong opinions, and of not taking responsibility when necessary – the cultivation of the cold and aloof position of a relativist'

(Cecchin 1987: 405). But this is certainly not what the Milan team meant by 'neutrality'.

Most therapists working with an individual have no difficulty in exploring their client's stories. What is more challenging is to extend the concept of neutrality to the important others in their life, particularly if they seem to be acting in an unfair or unpleasant way.

I attempted to be neutral towards Jonti's relationship with her husband and towards his behaviour by asking questions that could help me appreciate things from his point of view. 'If he were here, would he agree with that, or say something different?'

The therapist does not pretend to be impartial, but genuinely attempts to understand things from *everybody's* point of view. When we use systemic principles with an individual, we must attempt to do this with all the unseen others with whom the client is in relationship. Quite a tall order!

Jonti said that she had definitely decided to divorce her husband. I did not dissuade her from divorcing him or encourage her to divorce him, but explored their communication, the cultural meaning of divorce and its possible effect on all of them.

Importantly, 'neutrality' means not being prescriptive about the ways that a person (or a couple or family) ought to live. Being neutral as to the outcome of therapy also helps clients 'find their own preferred outcomes without imposing our own views on them' (Jones 1993: p. 102).

By exploring Jonti's relationships with her husband and her daughters, the relationship between her daughters and their father, and their relationships within the extended family, it became possible to momentarily take each of their positions and see how these fitted together.

When we work with an individual we can easily become caught up in the idea that their position is the 'correct' one. But we can avoid doing this when we use systemic perspectives.

I wanted to understand things from Jonti's husband's position, hear his 'voice': his attitudes to work and money and how these had affected the marriage and their family life. Attempting to be neutral towards his actions helped me not blame him, although her descriptions made him sound odious. After all, he was still the father of their children, who, she said, did love him.

Critiques of neutrality

The stance of neutrality has been critiqued for 'having a low level of indignation in the face of the terrible things humans do to each other' (Cecchin 1993). More worryingly, 'if we ignore the effects of societal inequities arising from a person's colour, race, gender and so on, we become trapped into a stance of *moral neutrality*' says Jones (1993: pp. 145–6).

With this in mind I explored the impact on Jonti of being a woman with much less earning power than her husband had. She had sacrificed a great deal to offer her daughters a good education and develop work opportunities for herself. I also connected with political stories in Nigeria. As we did this she began to celebrate the way she had survived numerous struggles as a woman, a mother and a wife, and was now involved in a major (exciting and daunting) life transition.

A therapist who ignores the effect of poverty, racism and so on on the client's life 'may be experienced . . . as implicitly and powerfully condoning their experiences of persecution . . .' (Boyd-Franklin 1989).

An invitation to curiosity

Cecchin (1987) responded to critiques of neutrality with the much richer concept, which he calls 'an invitation to curiosity'. One of the signs that shows that we are not being 'neutral', he says is when we get psychosomatic experiences such as headaches, perspiring, back pain and so on or when we become bored because we know for certain what is going on for the client. But by remaining constantly curious we can never be certain, because there are always more descriptions, connections and interactions going on that we are not aware of in the client's life (409–11). A stance of 'curiosity' helps us to question all our stories, theories, and responses. This is a stance of perpetual doubt.

I first showed my curiosity with Jonti by exploring the meanings she gave for saying that her husband was 'not a proper husband and father'. She described how he kept his money to himself, not using it for the family. I then became curious about their different attitudes to money. She wanted a man to support the family. His story was different.

Importantly, the idea of 'curiosity' encourages therapists to remain puzzled and questioning about our own reactions to clients. 'If we are curious, we question premises – our own and those of the . . . (client).' Indeed a client's 'interactions with us should facilitate questioning our own premises' (Cecchin 1987: 412).

Initially I had an intensely negative reaction to Jonti's husband as I had accepted the compelling story that she was a good wife and mother who was suffering because of her selfish husband. But as soon as I realised this I began to be curious about their relationship, the cultural and political climate in which they lived and his story. Circular (relationship) questions (explored in Chapter 6) helped me to see things from his position (and extended these questions to include other important people in their life). This allowed me to entertain alternative ideas; I did not want to alienate Jonti from her husband. After all, they had been together for 18 years, were still married, were negotiating a new kind of relationship and he was the father of their children.

By not being 'a true believer' we can then be free to be playful, to see the 'absurd aspects of the situation, as well as for the tragic' (Cecchin et al. 1992: p. 10).

Jonti told me that her husband's (dead) father had lived in poverty, feared it, and worked unrelentingly. Fearing poverty, Jonti's husband had become 'a workaholic', which was not 'normal' in their culture. Personal experience of redundancy then strengthened these ideas. But his way of life had cost him the love and approval of his extended family. This helped to co-create some very different ideas about him: he had put loyalty to his father's warnings above all else. Although she had 'known' these 'facts' about him, she was surprised that there could be a different way of viewing his behaviour. Also he was pretending that the marriage was still intact. Perhaps there was shame here? We began to talk in a more empathetic way about him. I became more curious about her father-in-law's life, the position of women in their culture, the meaning of work and money in their society as well as her family of origin, the way their marriage had been organised. He had lost a job some years before, which may have compounded this.

What can happen if we are not curious

Often systemic therapists assume that they understand the concept of curiosity, but their actions do not support this. An example of a therapist *not* showing curiosity about her favourite stories may illustrate this.

Jasbir's GP writes 'depressed' on the referral form to the practice counsellor/therapist. When she sees this she automatically connects to many societal and professional ideas about depression; Jasbir might be sleeping a lot, over or under-eating, find it difficult to do paid work, have relationship or financial problems and so on. Her Asian name might remind the therapist of recent news stories about enforced marriages. Jasbir is 23 and this makes her think about issues of identity. There might be dilemmas involving religion, culture, age and gender between her and her parents.

Before meeting Jasbir the therapist will, understandably, have developed many ideas about her, her family and her relationships.

When they meet, Jasbir tells her therapist (a white woman) that her parents want her to choose a Muslim husband, whilst she has a secret non-Asian boyfriend. The non-curious therapist becomes indignant on her behalf and encourages Jasbir to give more and more details about her critical and 'unfair' parents; the story strengthens. She does not explore their positions or other ideas; she has lost her curiosity.

Everything seems to confirm the idea that Jasbir is miserable because she cannot choose her future husband. The therapist encourages her to stand up for her 'rights' against her parents and believes that at her age she would be happier if she were more 'independent'. Jasbir continues to be sad and anxious about the future, although she looks forward to the sessions with her empathetic counsellor. After many weeks of discussion, Jasbir eventually leaves home to live with a friend; her relationship with her parents deteriorates. However, she is still unhappy and the therapist becomes exasperated and begins to believe the doctor's diagnosis of depression.

Cecchin et al. (1992: 58) write, 'Culturally it is quite easy for a therapist to experience himself [sic] as being a caring person without realizing that the caring can become pity, which in turn subtly implies a disrespectful attitude towards the client.'

Although the therapist was caring and empathetic towards Jasbir, she was not curious: she excluded everybody else's voice, the cultural and religious stories about arranged marriages and the cross-cultural stories that are being developed among second-generation British Asians. By doing so she exacerbated the differences between Jasbir and her parents.

Conversely when we are curious we learn information about the client and make connections that may have been missed had we simply been 'caring'. We make sense of the personal identity stories, the interactions between important people, and hear the stories that guide people's behaviours. And importantly, we notice the client's abilities and strengths as well as the abilities of the important people in their life.

The curious therapist would develop numerous ideas and ask questions to explore all the issues and explore the answers that the client gives in order to understand things from each person's position. Useful questions could be:

- Why do your parents think you have been finding it hard to get up?
- Who in the family would agree or disagree with them?
- Who in the community would agree/disagree with them?
- Whose idea was it for you to go to the doctor?
- What do your friends think about your boyfriend?
- If we could eavesdrop on a conversation your parents were having about your future, what might they be saying?
- How did your sister choose her husband?
- What dreams do your parents have about your future?
- What are the differences between the way Asian marriages are arranged in Britain from the way they are arranged in your parents' country?

The therapist could also explore relevant stories about:

- culture – differences and similarities between British and Asian cultures;
- religion – how it shows in this family;
- academic and employment success – what it means in this family;
- gender – differences and similarities between being a man and being a woman.

The curious therapist would reflect on the effect of the dominant Western idea that a 'love-marriage' is superior compared to the slower-growing love that may come from a successful arranged marriage. She would also challenge her own professional idea that 'individuating' from one's parents is always beneficial for a young person.

Showing irreverence to our prejudices

We all have prejudices. We cannot be free of prejudice. Cecchin (1992) says,

> In our profession, we hypothesise that personal premises influence the model of therapy that people choose. Prejudices are like heat-seeking missiles that home in on models that confirm pre-existing views of the world. In the therapy marketplace any prejudice can be developed into a theoretical model to be packaged and sold to prospective followers. (p. 52)

Systemic social constructionist approaches mean that we are able to employ a prejudice that is useful and form hybrids as we juxtapose other prejudices.

Jasbir's therapist was initially reverent to the prejudice that a love-match is preferable to allowing one's parents to find a suitable life-partner. She also had a prejudice that at a certain age a young woman must become 'individuated' from her parents.

However, 'Through the practice of irreverence, we will sometimes fail to honour, venerate, or even practise the axioms set forth by the various psychotheologies. Our work will instead be more organized by curiosity, desire, passion, imagination, invention, creativity, and improvization' (Keeney in Cecchin et al. 1992: p. x).

When we feel particularly strongly about our own ideas it is useful to ask ourselves how useful they are to the client. The more curious we are about our own stories the more we are more able to be irreverent to them (Cecchin 1992: pp. 9–10).

Honor, a therapist working in a hostel for young women, was seeing Trish, an 18-year-old white Scottish woman, single and now pregnant. In supervision Honor described becoming more and more alarmed because the hostel that catered only for single people was about to evict Trish and she appeared to have no family or friends.

When our clients appear to be 'stuck', it is likely that we too have become too reverent or 'stuck' on our own prejudices. However this is an invitation for us to become irreverent to them.

According to Honor, Trish was making no plans for when the baby was born. Clearly, this was a worrying situation.

By 'maintaining a continuous conversation with colleagues, people outside the mental health field, students and patients alike' we can become more irreverent to our dearly loved ideas say Cecchin et al. (1992: p. 9). However, when a therapist works alone it is important to tune into our own discomfort when the case is not progressing write Cecchin et al. (1994: p. 57). We all have our own warning signs that we are unable to be irreverent to one of our favourite stories or prejudices.

The tape of the session showed that Honor had become increasingly muddled and therefore unhelpful to Trish. Honor said that she had felt 'hot and dizzy'. This was useful information. She had lost the ability to be irreverent to her own prejudice that there was a certain way for a woman to prepare to give birth.

There is never one definitive account of what is going on. There are always many other ways of describing any situation.

The supervisor then became irreverent to the idea that Trish was irresponsible or helpless: she had been technically homeless for some time and had experienced more hardship than either of them. It was likely therefore that she had more personal resources and was more skilled than both of them realised.

'But it is at the moment when the therapist begins to reflect upon the effect of his [sic] own attitude and presumptions that he acquires a position that is both ethical and therapeutic' (Cecchin et al. 1992: p. 9).

How has Honor developed the idea that Trish was a helpless young woman? It was her slight build that made her feel maternal: she had recently become a grandmother and her daughter was now relying heavily on her. Honor felt helpless in the face of Trish's predicament. However, she had not made this connection during the session.

Honor and the supervisor began to be playful about the impending birth, making links to Mary and Jesus, giving birth in a stable, wise persons and so on. This was done in a respectful way and Honor recalled Trish's stories of strengths and personal resourcefulness that her prejudices had made her ignore.

It is important to appreciate, as Cecchin et al. say, that 'Not only are we intervening in their systems, but families are also intervening in our systems – helping us to become better systemic thinkers' (p. 412).

This in turn freed Honor up with her own daughter; when she talked to her she realised that she had survived the early months of the baby's life, she was much more competent than Honor had realised. At the following session with Trish she felt freer to ask many different questions that indeed showed that Trish had many amazing personal abilities. Also they discovered that a friend and a worker from the hostel would offer practical and emotional help.

Prejudices in themselves are not negative: 'prejudice is not necessarily unjustified and erroneous . . . prejudices are biases of our openness to the world' writes Gadamer (1987).

Honor's supervisor had a prejudice that a person who had negotiated the world of homelessness and hostels in London and the benefits system had many abilities and resources: it was likely that Trish was more skilled than Honor had appreciated. This prejudice enabled Honor to become more helpful to Trish.

Appreciating a client's resources connects to Lang and McAdam's (1995) stance of 'awe and engaged-amaze-ment' (102). This enables us to become irreverent to our own theories and stories. And, as Cecchin et al. (1992) say, 'You have to know something really well before you are able to be irreverent towards it.'

Irony to the discourse

Leppington (1991) suggests that we practise 'an ironic relationship to discourse-in-progress' (which) might better replace the 'stance of neutrality' often taken by therapists (79). This means critiquing the very way that theories which inform our work are assumed to be value-free but are often biased. For example Carole Gilligan's (1982) work revealed the inherent sexual bias in normative theories of human development. The stance of neutrality is particularly problematic 'in a context which seems to require radical social change, such as cases of rape or child abuse' or violence (Leppington 1991: 94).

Lena, a 20-year-old Swedish student, told me that she was unable to concentrate on her studies because of the effects of sexual abuse by her father. Moreover, she was in a perpetual state of fear since he was engineering opportunities to continue these acts. She considered making a disclosure to the police and dropping out of university. I did not show neutrality towards these inappropriate acts, which were severely affecting her every waking moment and preventing her from envisaging a good future.

MacKinnon and Miller (1987) write 'it may be those who lack an analysis of power relations who most easily, albeit unintentionally, engage in oppressive relationships' (p. 145).

We discussed how Lena's father had silenced her by dint of his enormous power: much loved in the family, a 'trusted' male authority figure with an elevated position in society, he had chosen to continue these violations. These ideas echoed those of a close older friend and Lena found them helpful.

'When therapists attend to experiences of inequity in the lives of their clients, they may worry that doing so constitutes taking a non-neutral stance,' writes Jones (1993: p. 147). However, when we do not speak out against inequality or abusive behaviour, this 'is likely to have the effect of (silently) condoning them, of giving the stamp of the therapist's authority ...'. It is therefore not a matter of 'whether to pay attention to power abuses, but how to work with them in a way that maximises the opportunities for change and choice of all members of the therapeutic system, including the therapist' (1993: p. 147).

We explored Lena's reasons for making a disclosure (to protect other children and young women) and the enormous ramifications for certain members of the family. I referred to McCarthy and Byrne's (1988) assertion that a young woman who takes a stand against sex abuse shows tremendous strength. She said that her friend had been urging her not to blame herself and if a professional had also said so, there may be something in this. This made me feel optimistic and hopeful. I was not neutral to all these issues.

Self-reflexivity and self–other-reflexivity

Reflexivity is one of the most useful concepts within systemic therapy says Burnham (1992: 17). Systemic social constructionist approaches require an ability to be constantly 'self-reflexive' about how our theories, prejudices and favourite stories inform our therapeutic work with our clients. Reflexivity is 'that which turns back upon, or takes account of itself ... (taking into account) the effect of the personality or presence of the researcher on the investigation' (*OED*: p. 476). This is not 'reflection' as in 'mirroring' (Anderson 1992: p. 67). McCarthy and Byrne (1990 in Burnham 1992: 25) describe reflexivity as 'meeting myself coming back . . . (and) arguing from a complementary position'.

As a psychiatric social worker I offered to visit Jim, a 45-year-old white man from London with a history of mental health difficulties, at his council flat, as his father had rung the psychiatrist to say that he was 'going downhill again'. 'Clinical depression' had brought him into hospital several times, but he had told his father that he was adamant that he was not going in again.

We must first be reflexive at the level of the theory we use (Burnham 1992).

I reflected on the theories about depression that abound in the mental health profession: some severe forms are thought to respond first (and only) to medication and hospitalisation. But professional experience helped me to be irreverent to this idea and to want to talk to Jim first.

When we are reflexive about the conversation as a whole, we consider whether a therapeutic conversation is actually useful at this time.

When Jim finally let me into the flat, I saw that he was sleeping on a mattress on the living-room floor; the flat was as unkempt as he himself was. He returned to the mattress and pulled the quilt over him.

We can be reflexive at the level of exploring an episode with a client: is this a useful episode to explore? And we can be reflexive when we explore the client's personal identity, family, gender, and ethnic and cultural stories.

I reflected on the fact that I was a professional woman visiting a 'depressed' man in his home and wondered what stories this act created for him. He told me that his father had told him that someone might come to see him.

We are self–other-reflexive about the language we use with the client and this affects them. Many professionals use 'public' language in front of clients says Anderson (1992) and a 'private' language that attracts 'nasty', 'intellectual', 'academic' . . . words and concepts' when they are not with the client (p. 58).

When I met Jim I did not privately think that his way of life was 'deficient' or abhorrent; I felt compassion and curiosity. I explained who I was and that I was there 'to help'; he nodded agreement that I could talk with him.

Social constructionist approaches claim that language is constitutive: it actually creates 'reality', therefore we must also be self-reflexive about the language that we use when we *think about* clients 'privately'. Self–other-reflexivity means that we 'watch like mad' (Lang 2003), by noticing our own emotional responses to the client and how this affects our style, pace and language. We also notice how the client responds to us, and then how we in turn respond to them.

Firstly I acknowledged my own powerful emotions at the way Jim appeared to be living. I felt great sorrow and empathy for him. I squatted on the floor beside him.

By oscillating between 'therapist' and 'observer' positions we can be fully absorbed in the conversation, but from time to time take more of an 'observer' position (Lang and McAdam 1995).

After a few minutes I momentarily took an observer position by listening to, and watching, my own language and responses. I noticed that I did most of the talking, asking questions and even using the technique of multiple choice questions: 'Do you agree with me, or am I talking rubbish?' Eventually I noticed that he would nod or communicate by using eye contact, looking at me, or away, or by closing his eyes.

Self–other-reflexivity helps us to perpetually reflect on the way the way our words and manner co-create reality in the moment-by-moment evolution of the conversation and our part in the process.

I asked Jim if it was still all right to talk and he said it was 'OK', which I took as encouragement to continue. After some time he told me that he had felt 'depressed' and hopeless since an important relationship had failed.

We must be constantly self-reflexive and vigilant in noticing how the client responds to us and then watch how we respond to them. This entails viewing the client as the expert and therefore taking what Anderson and Goolishian call a 'not knowing' approach (1992).

I did not assume that I 'knew' what was going on for Jim, but listened to the unique story he was telling me through his language: words, actions and demeanour. By being self–other-reflexive I noticed that as Jim responded to me I became a little more 'challenging'. He hesitantly confessed that his girlfriend had left because he preferred to spend his days in the pub. At this point he looked rather embarrassed.

Instead of 'not knowing' Lang and McAdam (1995) prefer the term 'learned not knowing' since it is impossible for us not to know certain things about people and the world in which we live.

I felt some frustration, but this was not the time or the place to show it. Instead I asked about his friendships, employment, money, his relationship with his father who lived on a nearby housing estate (his mother had died some years before). Jim said he had lost his job as a carpenter and was not confident about getting another. He was rather disparaging about his father and as he was becoming more fluent, and I did not want to risk alienating him, I decided not explore this relationship at this stage.

Systemic therapists who work with individuals can employ Anderson's (1990, 1992) inspiring idea of the 'reflecting team'. The reflecting team reversed the process of the one-way screen with the team talking about clients in private behind it, switching back and forth, so that clients can listen to the therapy team's conversation and the therapy team can listen to their conversation.

Now (imagining that I had a colleague from psychiatry with me), I mused aloud about the puzzling dilemma that Jim seemed to be in. Although he strongly maintained that did not want to be forced to go into hospital (again) under a section of the Mental Health Act, he was acting in such a way that this may be the doctor's only course of action. Jim agreed that he too was puzzled and was slightly aggrieved that his father had alerted the authorities. I was able to offer the idea that his father may be showing how much he cares about him.

Using reflecting-team ideas when we work alone helps us to offer numerous ideas and even contradictory points of view in a playful yet respectful way.

I noticed that Jim's initially downcast expression had softened and decided to try out the idea that some might say that he did in fact want to be 'cared for' in some way, and that being forced to go into hospital was a way for him to do this.

'In order to be able to attain this ability for self-reflexivity we believe that it is necessary to have a certain level of irreverence and a sense of humour' (Cecchin et al. 1992: p. 9).

Using a teasing tone I said 'So, you're a bit fed-up with your flat and your own cooking, and fancy a change of scenery and some nice hospital food?' He grinned briefly. I wondered if he had begun to consider the seriousness of what his actions were communicating. Jim agreed to come to my office to talk with me. When he did turn up this was a powerful communication to the doctors that he did not need to be hospitalised.

Reflecting-team principles are useful in helping those of us who work on our own, since supervision and other conversations about clients usually take place far from the context of the therapy. We can:

- regularly invite the client to give us feedback on their experience of the conversation;
- create joint notes with the client (Hedges 2000);
- share ideas from supervision and invite the client to respond to them;
- take these responses back to our supervisor as an ongoing reflecting conversation.

Self–other-reflexivity is particularly challenging for a therapist working alone. But getting into the habit of reflecting on our style, pace, ideas and language with the client, with peers, colleagues and supervisors can help us develop these practices and keep them alive. The results in terms of more ethical, open, effective and non-abusive therapeutic conversations are well worth while.

The 'fifth province'

A powerfully imaginative idea that helps us take multiple perspectives, invites curiosity in the therapist and a self-reflexive position is that of 'the fifth province' developed from ancient Celtic mythology (McCarthy 1994: 232). One account is that the 'fifth province' is a 'non-place'; another is that it was the 'fifth province' at the centre of Ireland where druids and

Celtic pagan priests resolved conflict through dialogue. For philosophers Helderman and Kearney (1982) this has 'come to represent a disposition towards tolerance and empathy'. McCarthy and Byrne (1988) use this metaphor in their work with sexually abused women and their families. By creating a space in which they can say the unsayable and think the unthinkable they develop creative ways of responding to the perpetrator of these actions. This enables a young woman to take charge of her life and not feel that she is a 'victim'.

With socially disadvantaged clients McCarthy says the 'fifth province' avoids professionals becoming 'colonised' by our theories (Freire 1972) and avoids potentially abusive language and practices. It enables therapists to hold together contradictory and often unequal positions and stories. It 're-includes a focus on marginal versions of reality and lifestyle . . . (it) does not entail a morally neutral stance on the part of the therapist. . . . rather it is a listening stance which does not aim to judge but to facilitate the emergence of accountability and responsibility in all participants . . . (and) an ethical stance in which the practitioner is open to the lived experiences of the person(s) she or he is encountering' (p. 233).

Overview of the metamorphosis of neutrality

- Neutrality (Selvini et al. 1980)
- Curiosity (Cecchin 1987)
- Irony (to the discourse) (Leppington 1991)
- Irreverence to our favourite stories (Cecchin et al. 1992)
- Multiple stories (Mendez and Maturana 1988)
- Questioning our prejudices (Cecchin et al. 1994)
- Self–reflexivity (Cecchin 1992; Hoffman 1992)
- Self–other-reflexivity (Lang 2003)
- 'Not knowing' (Anderson and Goolishian 1992)
- 'Learned not knowing' (Lang and McAdam 1995)
- The 'fifth province' (McCarthy and Byrne 1988)
- Awe, wonder and amaze-ment (Lang and McAdam 1995)

Developing self–other-reflexivity during the conversation we need to

- notice our emotional responses to the client;
- notice our physical responses to the client;
- notice the effect of our language (verbal and non-verbal) on the client;
- be curious about the theories that are guiding our work;
- explore with the client what meaning they give to our words and actions;
- ask the client what effect our ideas and questions have on them;
- question our own ideas (with colleagues and/or in supervision);
- notice new information that the client gives that refutes our ideas;
- notice when we become 'stuck';
- become irreverent towards our favourite ideas;
- be prepared to find other ideas if our favourite ones do not fit for the client;
- notice a client's resources and show awe and amaze-ment.

CIRCULAR QUESTIONING

Every behaviour is a communication which, in its turn, automatically provokes a feedback consisting of another behaviour-communication
                                                                        Watzlawick et al. (1967)

The concept of feedback can give a simpler and more consistent explanation of psychological data than does the psychical energy model
                                                                        Bowlby (1971)

To be human means to live a life immersed in social relationships
                                                                        Pearce (1994)

Working systemically with an individual client requires an imaginative leap. Circular (relationship) questions provide the tools that help us do this. The aim of this chapter is to help therapists use these questions effectively and elegantly. But they must be used within a *systemic* epistemology (way of thinking) rather than merely as a bolt-on set of techniques. And, whilst distinctions and taxonomies (Fleuridas et al. 1986; Tomm 1988) are extremely useful, McNamee (2003) says that these can seem to be like 'rules that we must follow'. This is certainly not the aim of systemic therapy. However, we must appreciate the revolution in communication theory that led to the Milan team's concept of 'circularity' from which these invaluable questions arose. The implications of this are still by no means accepted throughout the psychological and psychotherapeutic world.

The Milan team, inspired by Gregory Bateson's (1972) work with cybernetics and feedback, developed circular questioning, which enables therapists to enter the interpersonal systemic frame. Because these kinds of questions are always to do with relationships of one kind or another we sometimes prefer to talk about 'relationship questions'. Also, although we use the term 'circularity', it is more helpful to think of a spiral. As Fleuridas et al. (1986) say 'asking these kinds of questions can help the client (and therapist) move to a different position, whereas the concept of circularity implies a return to the same point.' These questions are crucial in enabling us to retain *curiosity* and we cannot know which circular questions to ask unless we have a *systemic* hypothesis. Although the three concepts are intimately interrelated, we must put off a discussion of hypothesising until the next chapter.

Angela, a 37-year-old white woman, tells me that she feels depressed. I resist the urge to search for the 'cause' of her 'depression' or to only explore her internal world, which would separate her from the important people in her life. Instead, I listen acutely for any connection that she makes with an important person, so that together we can make sense of how the description of 'depression' came to be made.

In order to do this I imaginatively:

(1) *visualise* her connected to people who are significant to her;
(2) listen for these people's influential *voices*;
(3) connect with the powerful *emotions* they all feel.

She may be in close daily relationships with certain people or separated in time or geography from them; or they may be no longer living. The voices may be tiny unheard whispers or strong insistent ones. Her feelings may be clear or hard to put into words.

I will outline Angela's story making connections with the theoretical foundation of circularity, interweaving particular 'circular questions'.

Using a genogram to map relationships

Relationships, for human beings (as for all mammals) wrote Bateson (1972) are our primary form of existence. Before our birth we are physically dependent on our mother for our life. We are born into pre-existing complex networks of relationships that we did not choose; we depend on these relationships for physical, emotional and social sustenance and this has ramifications for the rest of our lives (Pearce 1994: p. 216).

Angela begins by telling me that she is afraid that her 15-year marriage is suffering because of 'her depression'. I do not at this stage focus on 'depression', but try to map the important relationships in her life. So with her help I draw:

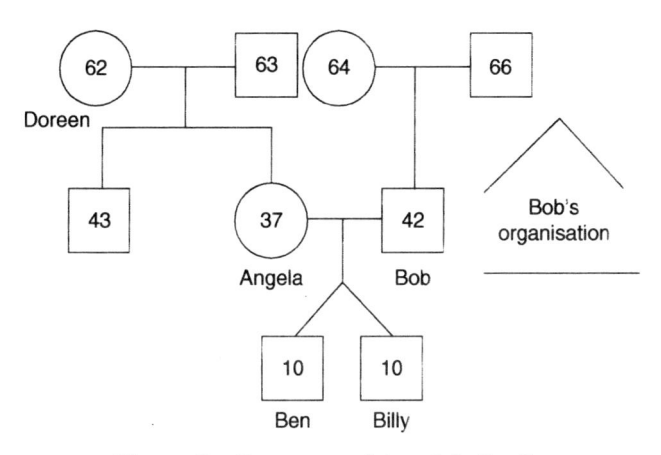

Figure 2 Genogram of Angela's family

a *genogram/family tree* showing her family, friends, any significant professionals, organisations and so on (see Figure 2).

Systemic therapists are interested in the stories that clients tell about family relationships because the family (or an equivalent) is the crucible in which we develop our identities and learn about how the world operates. 'The patterns of conversations within families are . . . the most important in our social worlds' writes Pearce (1994: p. 311) and the family is 'the primary and, except in rare instances, most powerful system in which we humans ever belong' (McGoldrick et al. 1999: 2–3). These early patterns of conversations including significant non-kin relationships form the backdrop of language, values and stories for future relationships.

Gradually as Angela and I talk the room metaphorically becomes filled with the important people in her life, and their patterns of interaction.

Genograms become 'an important way of joining, and a way of showing the interconnectedness of relationships with families' (McGoldrick et al. 1999: 2–3). This can be more powerful for individual clients who may come with the Western idea that individuals are discrete beings and for therapists who do not find it easy to think in a relational way. When we draw a genogram with a client, as well as putting in blood/family connections, we add significant friends and professionals: some people's relationships with probation officers or social workers can be highly influential. Important relationships with the broader community and relevant institutions such as schools, work contexts and so on must be acknowledged. And factual details about occupation can be invaluable.

Angela says that her husband Bob works for an organisation that has become dominant in their marriage; since loyalty is synonymous with working long hours, this has created dilemmas for them.

Information about what we refer to as the GRRAACCCES: gender, race, religion, age, abilities. class, culture, colour, ethnicity and sexual orientation, can be crucial (Burnham 1992).

Bob's parents are British and not religious, but Angela's family, originally farmers from southern Ireland, are Catholic. There are many differences in values between them. Work is an important context here: Angela's parents had hoped that she would marry a man who could give her a better standard of life than the one they had. Bob however, has rejected some of his parents' 'materialistic' values and works for a charity at a fairly low salary.

Genograms enable us to explore myths, rules, emotionally charged issues of previous generations, repetitive patterns, illnesses, shifts in family relationships, critical life changes and possible connections between personal identity and family and cultural events over time say McGoldrick et al. (1999: 2–3). Also the genogram can be viewed from multiple perspectives, such as from a sister's, brother's, grandparents' point of view and so on.

I start to map the connections Angela has with significant others by asking her:

- *who is closest to whom;*
- *what similarities and differences there are between them.*

Angela says she is closest to her mother, but her marriage is different from her parents' traditional one: until recently she and Bob always shared the domestic chores and the care of their ten-year-old twin boys Ben and Billy.

When we work with an individual who comes with psychological explanations for their (or others') behaviour, drawing a genogram can help both of us make systemic connections and 'provides a ready vehicle for systemic questioning which, in addition to providing information for the clinician, begins to orient the (client) ... to a systemic perspective (and) see the larger picture' (McGoldrick et al. 1999: 2–3). This can be used in a creative way by including non-biological relationships, places, organisations and so on.

Certain events may have affected Angela, so I may also draw:

a *time line* of events.

She tells me that when she was made redundant, some months ago, things changed at home.

A time line can help both the therapist and the client to notice:

- times when certain people were *closer*;
- times when they were *less close*;
- *when* and *with whom* Angela feels more unhappy;
- *when* and *with whom* she feels happier.

She says that Bob and the children enjoyed having her at home; then Bob began to relinquish the bulk of the household chores and the childcare. As everybody began to get used to this Angela resented it more and more. And it created some tension with her mother, as we shall see.

The circular questions that we ask can help us make *connections* and distinctions between how:

- Angela describes the *future*, the *present* and the *past*;
- how Bob and others describe the *future*, the *present* and the *past*.

Although Bob was 'generous', Angela began to resent her lack of financial independence. And her identity changed: where she had once enjoyed describing herself as 'a secretary' (as well as a wife and a mother) she began to call herself 'just a housewife' (a derogatory term in her eyes). Imperceptibly she lost contact with colleagues: her professional dreams evaporated and she stopped looking for another job.

Circular questions undermine the client's belief system by using the language of relationship, not of 'what is'. These questions imply pattern not 'facts' and help us to move away from viewing ideas as products of the internal world to patterns and interaction says Cecchin (1987: 412). Human beings create patterns all the time says Bateson (1972). These questions help us begin to make sense of how each person responds within:

- certain *conversations*;
- particular sequences of *actions*;
- specific places and *contexts*.

Angela responded to my questions telling me that as Bob began working longer hours he began to help less in the home. He was often tired; their sex life diminished and Angela began to feel less and less attractive. Bob seemed to be withdrawing emotionally and now became irritable. Angela became concerned about the marriage and felt that she was a failure 'even as a housewife'. She often cried when she was alone. To cap it all the boys began to 'play up'. Angela became stricter with them; she demanded that Bob back her up. His parenting style was more laid back and they began to argue. She turned to her mother, Doreen, and would often cry uncontrollably. Doreen did not agree with her daughter's expectations of Bob but was reminded of a time when she had been unhappy with her husband and been given antidepressants; she urged Angela to see the doctor. The doctor referred her for counselling.

The conventions involved in writing may make this appear to be a *linear* development of events and responses, but my intention is to show the complex *patterns* of communications in which they were all involved. Watzlawick et al. (1967) showed in their research with people diagnosed 'schizophrenic' (a term used differently from the way it is used today) that an individual's behaviour could appear bizarre when they were seen on their own, but would make perfect sense when they were seen with their families. If I had focused primarily on Angela (and her 'depression'), we would have missed an enormous amount of information that could make sense of all their actions, thoughts and feelings. So I metaphorically worked from her position *and* from the multiple positions of her husband, her sons *and* her mother: an interpersonal frame.

Angela began to recognise how she and Bob were each affected by what they believed the other was communicating and were simultaneously affecting each other's behaviour: a complex patterning of communications. Gradually her original description of herself as a woman with an intrapsychic problem called 'depression' began to lose potency.

Systemic thinking liberates us from pathologising individuals by showing that problems are co-created within conversations between people. It made sense to work with the interaction between Angela and her immediate family, but some clients' significant relationships are less easy to identify.

They may *appear* at first to have few or none. However, as we recall, being human means that we are social beings, with the propensity to form relationships.

Donald, a 55-year-old man from Glasgow, who has been sleeping rough for years, maintains that he is 'a loner'. However, he does live within a society; he may be (however loosely) connected to workers in a day centre or a night shelter and be part of an informal network of friends with similar lifestyles. He will communicate directly or in a convoluted way with all these people, who will in turn respond to him, and so on. Donald was once a child; he would have had intimate relationships and/or been part of some kind of 'family' structure even if he had been brought up in care. He may have worked or have been married. He certainly lives within a cultural landscape with values and beliefs that affect him and are affected by his actions or even non-actions. And as soon as we meet Donald we become part of his interpersonal network.

In this way 'interpersonal systems, families . . . even international relationships etc – may be viewed as feedback loops.' These 'require a philosophy of their own in which concepts of *pattern* and *information* are as essential as those of matter and energy were at the beginning of this century' (Watzlawick et al. 1967: 31–2).

However, in my experience, therapists do not find it easy for to shift from the familiar individualistic explanatory frame to one that involves feedback and pattern-like descriptions. There are two main conceptual reasons for this:

(1) the way that psychology and psychoanalysis drew their fundamental concepts from science;
(2) the very way our language is constructed.

Before exploring these issues I look at how the Milan team were influenced by Gregory Bateson (1972) and Shands (1971) to critique these major tenets.

A revolution in communication theory

Bateson translated Weiner's (1947) concept of cybernetics and feedback loops into human interaction. And Bateson's 'systemic' ideas about communication were 'brilliantly articulated as a set of practices for family therapists' by the Milan team says Pearce (1994: p. 236), the most important of which is circular questioning, 'a remarkably powerful and adaptable way of moving around relationships'.

I worked with the 'feedback loops' between Angela and the others in her life, how they respond to each other in highly complex ways.

Bateson (1972) used these ideas to show that 'the individual mind is . . . also in pathways and messages outside the body' (p. 461). So we are interested in the ways that our client's actions and their ideas about others are seen in the ways in which they act with each other, in the 'observable manifestations of relationship' (Watzlawick et al. 1967).

So I ask Angela circular (relationship) questions. 'If the twins were here how would they describe things between you and their father right now?' This begins to connect her 'internal' stories with the 'observable manifestations' of their relationships.

Instead of looking to the individual (with 'the problem') who if seen in isolation could *appear* to be behaving in pathological ways, the Milan team worked with whole families and the co-evolving patterns of feedback between them. 'From the beginning of systems thinking' writes Jones (1993: p. 20) 'cybernetics is fundamental to the way family therapists have tried to understand the circularity of organisation in family patterns.'

No matter how much we knew about Angela (or others in her life) in advance, we could never predict the effect that her redundancy would have on her. Nor could we predict how increased responsibilities at work would affect Bob, or their sex life nor whether this would affect Angela, the twins, her mother and so on. Angela, Bob, her mother and the boys will each have a certain number of stories from which they will draw when making meaning for their own and each other's responses. When her sons 'play up' Angela may refer to a personal story about her ability to be a good mother.

Information is difference: difference is a relationship

As we have seen, we are all born into relationships. Bateson inspired the Milan team to employ the interrelated concepts of difference and relationship:

- The brain processes 'information' as 'difference'.
- Any difference implies a relationship.
- Human communication is based on perceptions of difference.

Human communication occurs in a domain of difference because of the way brain processes information; all knowledge of external events is derived from 'difference', which can be in:

- touch;
- hearing;
- vision.

Bateson (1972) says 'to achieve more accurate perception, a human being will always resort to change in the relationship between himself and the external object.' For example, when we touch a rough spot on some surface we move our finger over the spot, 'thus creating a shower of neural impulses with definite sequential structure' (Bateson 1972: p. 452). This helps us work out the hardness, shape, texture, and so on. Similarly, 'a steady unchanging sound is difficult to perceive and may even become unnoticeable' (Watzlawick et al. 1978: p. 27). There needs to be a slight variation for a sound to be 'heard'. Also there must be some distinction, however slight, for us to see something, since 'when by an ingenious device, eye movement is made impossible so that the same image continues to be perceived by the same areas of the retina, clear visual perception is no longer possible' (Watzlawick et al. 1967: p. 27).

Angela says that she had noticed a change in Bob in that he is more tired in the evenings, less helpful and less attentive. Maybe his feelings for her have changed; perhaps Bob finds her less attractive since she has put on a bit of weight? Angela sees a relationship between Bob's behaviour and her body shape: a strong story in our culture. He, however, may not make this distinction.

'A process of change, motion, or scanning is involved in all perception. In other words, a relationship is established' (Watzlawick et al. 1978: p. 28). All knowledge of external events is derived from the relationship between them; what we perceive easily is difference and change – and difference is a relationship (Bateson 1972).

What is important for us is that in the world of communication we are in a world in which 'differences' create 'effects' and difference is always seen as creating a relationship (Bateson 1972: p. 452). Very often people notice some distinctions and differences in their lives, but not others; and circular questions target perceptions of difference (not 'facts') says Pearce (1994: p. 237). So they are immensely useful in helping clients to hear what Bateson (1972) calls 'news of difference' or 'a difference which makes a difference' (p. 453).

In order to connect with Angela's perception of the 'difficulties' in her sex life with Bob (having the idea that a married couple's sex life ebbs and flows depending on what is going on), we could ask questions that target difference. 'When did you first notice that there was something different going on in your sex life?' 'Were there other times in your marriage when you and Bob were less active sexually?' 'Were there times when you were more sexually active?' 'Do you think you are different or similar to other couples who have been married for 15 years?'

Bateson (1972: p. 452) writes, 'In the world of mind, nothing – that which is not – can be a cause ... The letter which you do not write can get an angry reply; and the income tax form which you do not fill in can trigger the Internal Revenue ... into energetic action.'

When Bob comes home late from work his very absence is a communication, although we cannot be sure what the communication 'means' and whether he is aware of what he may be communicating to Angela.

Even silence or an apparent non-response is a communication: we cannot *not* communicate.

If Bob does not ring Angela to tell her that he will be late or if Angela is not home when Bob gets in, these are communications.

Language is linear: life is circular and dynamic

Because our language is 'linear' it creates the idea of linear causality says Shands (1971). Systemic therapy challenges this assumption by distinguishing between the way we talk about our relationships with others and so on with the way that they actually unfold and develop in the world. Language distinguishes between a 'subject' and an 'object', a person who *performs* the action and the person who *receives* the action, a 'before' and an 'after', and this creates an assumption that the world is organised in the same linear way.

Angela says that she began to feel 'depressed' after losing her job, or because Bob is doing less around the house, or because his job takes him away from home a lot, and this explains why the twins have become rude or difficult.

But the world of actions and interaction is much more complex.

The very words Angela uses have created some kind of order out of the multiple stories and the maelstrom of confused feelings in the family. The therapist must not get caught in simple cause and effect created by 'linguistic conditioning'. There may, of course, be some kind of connection between Angela losing her job and Bob doing less domestically, but we cannot know how this works unless we explore the unique connections between these events and each person's responses.

Shands' critique of the 'tyranny of linguistic conditioning' inspired the Milan team to shift from a 'linear and causal epistemology' to a more systemic one. 'Language is not reality, the former is linear while the latter is living and circular . . . the living system (is) dynamic and circular, and the symbolic system (language) . . . is descriptive, static and linear' (Selvini et al. 1978: pp. 51–2).

Language 'makes us think that the universe is organized on a linear basis, in cause and effect patterns' says Shands (1971); but 'we soon learn that in any delicate and complicated context we cannot find such a concretely defined order except by imposing it' (p. 32). However, 'Each time we try to explain our behaviour', Cecchin (1987: 406) writes, 'we typically find causal descriptions the most satisfying'.

If Bob is late home Angela may ask him 'Why?' The logical response to a 'why' question is 'because'. Bob may give an explanation: 'because I had to finish off the report before tomorrow'. This could end the conversation. But it may be more complex than that.

'The problem' Shands (1971: pp. 19–20) says 'is words. Only with words can man [sic] become conscious; only with words learned from another can man learn to talk to himself. Only through getting the better of words does it become possible for some, a little of the time, to transcend the verbal context and to become, for brief instants, free.' Since words are the tools that we use in our work, we can, Pearce (1989: p. 84) says 'treat words and language as "friends" instead of "masters" or "slaves"'. By being playful with words and their meanings, using humour and irony (in a respectful way of course) we can 'transcend the verbal context'.

If Angela says in a disparaging tone of voice that Bob had begun to change into a 'typical man', I could use a humorous tone to play with the notion of 'typical man' or the idea that he is 'changing' (like Superman in reverse). I could ask her what 'typical man' means, when did she notice the changes, were they subtle or sudden? Did Bob fool her for 15 years before showing Angela that he was, after all, a 'typical man'? Could it be something to do with his age – or perhaps something else? Is he turning into his own father (continuing with the idea of 'change')? Would he agree? Who else would agree/disagree? Does he like (or dislike) this? If you had known 15 years ago that Bob would become a 'typical man' would you have married him? If Bob continues to become more and more typical, how will he be in five years' time? Or perhaps we could playfully make the distinction between 'typical man' and 'new man'.

From 'to be' to 'to show'

The Milan team (Selvini et al. 1978, 1980) replaced the verb 'to be' with the verb 'to show', elegantly avoiding the 'tyranny of linguistic conditioning' and showing that 'appearance is not necessarily reality'. 'What we say *about* a person is in effect... no more than a function of the relationship' (Selvini et al. 1978: p. 26). 'Avoiding the authoritative verb "to be"', Cecchin (1987: 412) writes, 'helps us to overcome linear explanations'. 'The verb *to be* condemns us to think according to the linear model... to postulate that a causality exists.' 'In order not to become trapped by the idea that there exists some kind of intrapsychic reality, we had to force ourselves to systematically substitute the verb *to seem* or *to show* for the verb *to be*' (Selvini et al. 1978: pp. 26–7).

If a client *appears* sad, instead of believing that he or she *is* sad (seeing sadness as something she 'possesses' or as an intra-psychic reality), then wondering 'Why is she sad?' (leading to *explanations* for 'her sadness'), we could hypothesise about what this *shows* (as a communication) and the meaning of this.

I could explore the idea that maybe Angela wants to show Bob that she misses his involvement around the house, or that she would like him to become more affectionate. I could ask Angela: 'When you feel sad or unhappy how do you show it?' Angela may reply, *'I cry.'* The following shows circular questions in action:

Therapist: *'When was the last time you cried?'*
Angela: *'After Bob went to work last Monday'.*
Therapist: *'Did anybody know that you cried then?'*
Angela: *'My mother knew.'*
Therapist: *'How did she know?'*
Angela: *'I rang her.'*
Therapist: *'What idea did she have for why you had been crying?'*
Angela: *'She says its because I'm depressed.'*
Therapist: *'If the tears could speak, what would they be saying?'*
Angela: *(long pause) 'I want to be comforted.'*
Therapist: *'Who would you most want to hear say that?'*
Angela: *'Bob'.*

Notice that the therapist does not ask about how Angela *feels* 'inside'. Systemic therapists are certainly interested in clients' feelings, but we are even more interested in their crucial communication and interactional patterns, and how their feelings and emotions have been co-created within their relationships.

Circular questioning undermines the client's 'belief system' says Cecchin (1987) 'by using the language of relationship, not of "what is"' which is often 'based on "truths" and the heavy usage of the verb "to be" ("My son is lazy"; "my daughter is stubborn"; "my father is an alcoholic")' (412).

If Angela says her son 'Ben is rude', or has 'become more rude' we can ask 'How does he show his rudeness?', 'What does he do that gives you the idea that he is rude?' or 'Who notices his rudeness?' This immediately gets us into an interpersonal frame. Angela may say that he swore at her. Not only does this give us invaluable information about Ben's behaviour, but by asking 'What word did he use?', 'Where were you?', 'What was happening before he said it?', 'What did you say/do then?' we begin working with the interactions between them. Importantly it gets us away from blaming Ben or seeing his 'rudeness' as some attribute that he possesses. We could ask, 'When he shows this rude behaviour, what else could he be wanting to communicate?' or 'If his father were here now what would he say Ben was trying to express?'

Punctuation

Ideas from cybernetics show us that no one person or event unilaterally 'leads' or 'steers' things in human interaction. A systemic circular view of human interaction does not assume an initial cause, or at any rate does not see it as essential to the understanding of the current pattern. However, what we describe as the starting point of a sequence of events will create some order in what is an unstructured stream of life events.

Angela's mother may describe Bob as being the one who 'steers' the marriage, whereas it may be more difficult to say which one is the 'leader' and which one is the 'follower'.

'From a strictly circular and systemic perspective any punctuation in the sense of before and after, cause and effect, can only be arbitrary' (Selvini et al. 1978: p. 40).

Coming to talk with a therapist is a major punctuation in Angela's life. And by asking Angela how she decided to come to make the appointment it is not so much that we seek the 'true reason', but want to make sense of how she came to make the decision.

In a long sequence of interchange, people tend to punctuate the sequence so that it will appear that one person or another has taken the initiative, or is dependent on another's actions. 'They will set up patterns (about which they may or may not be in agreement)' which perpetuate and reinforce the other's actions (Bateson and Jackson in Watzlawick et al. 1967: p. 56).

We could ask who else knows that she decided to come to talk, who would be surprised and so on, which begins to create a systemic conversation. We may provisionally accept Angela's initial 'punctuation' that she felt low after losing her job. However, if we ask circular questions such as 'If your mother were here what would she say is the reason for you feeling so low?' Angela may say 'Oh, she'd say it was when Bob got a new job that meant he was hardly ever at home.' Neither is more 'correct': just a different punctuation.

'Disagreement about how to punctuate the sequence of events is at the root of countless relationship struggles' write Watzlawick et al. (1967: p. 56). 'To an outside observer, a series of communications can be viewed as an uninterrupted sequence of interchanges (but) the participants in the interaction always introduce ... "the punctuation of the sequence of events"' (p. 54).

If we ask Angela what Bob would say was the 'cause' of their diminished sex life she may say that he would say that she had rebuffed his advances one time. But her best friend might say that she did this after a humorous remark Bob had made about her weight.

But any punctuation is an 'arbitrary' one, 'which isolates such behaviour from the ... context of preceding behaviours which can be traced back to infinity' (Selvini et al. 1978: p. 5). 'Over time members of a family come to form predictions, not only of each other's actions, but also of each other's thoughts, beliefs and feelings ... they come to form a web of mutual anticipation' (Dallos and Draper 2000: p. 70).

Bob, Angela, her mother, the twins will each respond to the other's actions and behaviours, creating meaning out of what the other says and does.

The way things are described very much depends on who is doing the telling, who 'punctuates' the story and where it is 'punctuated'. But critiquing the 'stimulus-response psychologist' who only 'looks at extremely short sequences' Bateson and Jackson (in Watzlawick et al. 1967: pp. 54–5) say that 'the sequences of interchange are actually much longer, since every action involved in any sequence is simultaneously stimulus, response and reinforcement'.

If Angela's mother responds to her daughter's 'depression' by visiting more often, the twins may enjoy this and talk about her more; Angela may be grateful to her but feel redundant. This may reinforce her idea that she is not a good mother, If she, tearfully, tries to explain this to Bob he may see this as showing that she needs professional help. Each person may have a different set of stories: Bob may say that Angela is like her mother in being easily dissatisfied with life: he married a potential 'depressive'; Angela's best friend may say that Angela is dissatisfied with her marriage and that Bob is jealous of her girlfriends. The doctor may say that Angela has a propensity for depression, because of her inherited biology.

None of these is 'correct' as a stand-alone 'explanation': in a systemic approach we recognise that many stories are interconnected and involve highly complex interactions and that there is no simple causality in human communication processes.

Bateson says 'the dilemma arises out of the spurious punctuation... namely that it has a beginning, and this is precisely the error of the partners in such a situation' (in Watzlawick et al. 1967: p. 59). While in linear chains of causality (as in the sciences) it is meaningful to speak of about the beginning and end of a chain, these terms are meaningless in systems with feedback loops. There is no beginning and no end to a circle: we simultaneously influence other people, whilst reacting to their behaviour.

The therapist is also part of the 'circle'

We must now take yet another imaginative leap: when a therapist works primarily with the *client's* patterns of interaction (as we have done in this example), this implies that we can be 'objective' outsiders. However, scientists and philosophers from many different disciplines came to recognise that such objectivity is impossible. Selvini et al. (1980) were already aware of this: 'By circularity we mean the capacity of the therapist to conduct his [sic] investigation on the basis of feedback form the family in response to the information he solicits and, therefore, about difference and change.'

My ideas and stories about 'depression', marriage, families, what is 'normal' behaviour for a working wife and mother in this society, and for a married man, a working husband and father and so on, will inform what questions and comments I make as I listen to Angela.

This idea was described as 'second-order cybernetics', 'the view that reality invariably involves a construction, occurs in relationships and is based on feedback' write Dallos and Draper (2000: p. 13). And 'Rather than thinking that we could observe and analyse families in any detached and objective manner it became increasingly clear that the therapist/observer inevitably perturbed or changed the family system by the very act of observing it' (p. 73).

The language I use, the way I talk with Angela, the stories and ideas I have about 'depression', marriage, sex and so on will influence my language (verbal and non-verbal) and this will shape the conversation. Our conversation will affect the way Angela describes herself, and how she responds to Bob, the twins, her mother, her friends and the doctor.

Also, all our actions, including the language we use, occur within a particular cultural societal context. For example we cannot overlook the gender stories that we draw on, what we think it means to be a man, a husband, a father, a wife, woman, mother and a daughter and so on. The power of these stories is described in the following chapter on hypothesising.

Circular/relationship questions seek information about differences between

- *People*: 'Who notices most when you feel low?'
- *Behaviour*: 'Who is most rude, Billie or Ben?'
- *Events*: 'Did Bob do more around the house before he got promotion or before you were at home more?'
- *Relationships*: between all the above

What circular questions do

Circular questions are invaluable in enabling therapists to think relationally and therefore systemically, and enable therapist and client develop new connections. They:

- broaden the frame from the individual to interaction;
- shift from 'linear' cause-effect to interaction;
- demonstrate the importance of relationship;
- bring forth unheard voices;
- make connections between the meaning of important events;
- make links between the present, future hopes and past stories;
- keep therapists' curiosity alive;
- help the client become more curious about their life;
- enable us to 'test out' and refute hypotheses;
- introduce 'news of difference';
- open space for new connections;
- enable therapists to respect the client as the expert in their life;
- change the stories.

7

HYPOTHESISING AND SYSTEMIC STORY CREATION

Just as it is impossible not to communicate, it is also impossible not to have a hypothesis
Cecchin et al. (1992)

When we impose our own view of the world upon those we invade (we) inhibit the creativity of the invaded by curbing their expression
Freire (1972)

We usually tell our students, 'You should keep in mind 24 hypotheses, 50 stories'
Cecchin (1992)

'Hypothesising is the most important aspect of systemic work' says Lang (2003). This is because the explanations we connect with and the descriptions we use as we work with each client will profoundly influence how we respond to them. The ability to do systemic hypothesising requires a through understanding of the systemic principles (neutrality/curiosity, positive connotation, and circularity) described in the preceding chapters. These concepts provide the foundation for developing hypothesising skills.

We all create hypotheses in our daily life: we constantly make conjectures, have hunches, and create meanings and stories in order to make sense of the world. When we do any kind of therapeutic work with people these ideas affect how we respond to the client. 'As we shifted our focus to ourselves', Cecchin et al. (1992: p. 90) write, 'we became aware that we always had a hypothesis in mind'. And 'whenever we say something to the client we reveal our own ideas.' These ideas, assumptions and so on powerfully influence what we notice and what we ignore in the conversation. And this affects our mannerisms and gestures, tone of voice and the words we use, which in turn will affect the way the client comes to describe themselves and their life.

De Shazer (1991, 1993), the solution-focused therapist, has famously questioned the ethics of hypothesising saying that if he feels a hypothesis coming on he lies down until it goes away. But Lang and McAdam (1995) say that we always have hunches and ideas that we follow and explore, whether we admit to doing this or not. 'We would say that his whole approach to therapy is based on a series of global hypotheses or stories – namely that the solution predates the problem and exceptions to the problem are open to view' they say (p. 78).

Andy was one of four therapists who were co-creating hypotheses about Brenda, a 33-year-old white British woman after Brenda's first session with Nilu, her new therapist. Her previous therapist at another place had left without explanation and she wanted to continue to explore her relationship with her manager. Andy mused aloud that Brenda must have been feeling angry, distressed and abandoned, especially since her father had died when she was young.

However there was no indication that she was experiencing emotions related to the 'loss' of her previous therapist. 'When we hypothesise we do not seek to fit clients' stories into prescribed stories or theories' write Lang and McAdam (1995: p. 77).

Because Brenda had clearly connected to Nilu we could instead hypothesise about Brenda's ability to be open to her new therapist.

Because the aim of systemic therapy is to work as briefly and elegantly as possible, hypothesising is not something that we should skip, since it 'guides the therapist's activity, keeping it from becoming random' (Jones 1993: p. 14). Lang and McAdam's (1995) term 'systemic story creation' is a more apt description of the hypothesising process and moves us away from the scientific connotation, although 'systemic story *co*-creation' is perhaps better since this acknowledges the way we always co-construct reality in conversation *with* each client. I will use these terms interchangeably.

Systemic hypothesising helps us to articulate and elucidate our meanings, stories, conjectures and so on in a deliberate way. Exploring a working hypothesis helps us to:

- connect more closely to the client's unique stories;
- work with the client's significant relationships;
- see 'everybody as doing the best they can given all the circumstances';

- become more creative and flexible by entertaining many descriptions;
- become more curious and self–other-reflexive;
- prevent meandering conversations;
- do more effective brief work;
- become alert to the danger of imposing our view of the world onto the client.

This last point is important since 'Society', write Lang and McAdam (1995) 'invests a great deal of power in the healing professions . . . (and) taking time to hypothesise before, during and after every interaction with a client gives the therapist . . . time to consider issues of power' (p. 79).

'When we hypothesise we stick to the details and the focus and frame of what the person is talking about; we stick to their language and the things they raise' says Lang (2003).

Had Brenda been reluctant to talk, referred to her previous therapist, or talked about a loss-related theme, then Andy's hypothesis may have been useful. But because he was attuned to abandonment as an important therapeutic story he 'heard' the story of loss, rather than Brenda's main concerns about her job.

Each client 'is going to be different', says Cecchin (Boscolo et al. 1987: p. 164) and 'every time you make . . . a hypothesis, it should be checked and questioned. Otherwise, you create constructs similar to analytic therapy where you look for oedipal complexes, paranoia and so forth.'

Of course the therapist cannot 'not know' the information about Brenda's previous therapist and her father's death, but because these losses are not her current focus, it would be an imposition to work with a hypothesis that foregrounds loss.

We constantly check our hypotheses by asking questions, and observing the client's responses; as soon as one idea does not fit or resonate for the client we must jettison it. However hypothesising can be challenging. Partly, writes Cecchin (1987: 412), this is because 'The history of the western world is characterized by the pursuit for accurate explanations. With such a history, it is no surprise that we all find it difficult to generate hypotheses, which requires suspending the search for one explanation.'

Andy's hypothesis did not resonate with Brenda's major issues or her language (words or manner).

'The refutation of a hypothesis', says Jones (1993: p. 14) 'is not considered a failure, but is seen as furthering understanding' and helps us to avoid the search for an explanation (or truth statement). Indeed, as Cecchin (1992: p. 90) says, 'The value of a hypothesis is not in its truth but in its ability to create a resonance (a combination of body messages, verbal utterances, ideas and hypotheses) with those involved.'

The issues that did resonate for Brenda concerned her career and her relationship with her manager.

We could begin to hypothesise that concerns about her job and her future were currently those she wanted most to resolve. 'When we hypothesise we look for understandings that help us make sense of the coherence of people's actions' (Lang 2003). When we impose our ideas on them we do a great disservice to our clients.

Brenda told Nilu about the competitive ethos of the organisation she worked for and the therapeutic team were curious about the 'logic' that told her 'you must stick things out even if they are unpleasant.' We may notice that Brenda is developing many abilities in this context: tenacity, negotiation skills and so on.

We 'develop a sense of awe, wonder and respect for the uniqueness of the client and their system' write Lang and McAdam (1995: 77).

We may be curious about how the ethos of the organisation manifests in the relationship between Brenda and her manager. We may also wonder about the personal, identity, family and professional stories that Brenda is connecting with in this context.

If we draw these preliminary ideas as a mind map, the connections can be made visually, which can be a more vivid way to carry ideas with us into the next conversation (see Figure 3).

Where do hypotheses come from?

Hypotheses, say Boscolo et al. (1987: p. 163) draw from four sources:

- data (information about, and from, the client);
- theory – our professional theories;

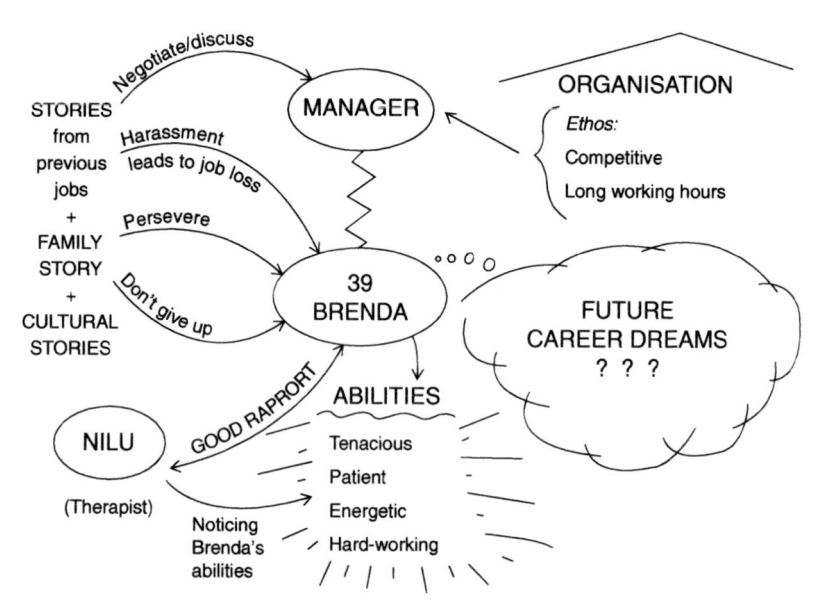

Figure 3 Mindmap: making connections when hypothesising

- our experience of working with many clients;
- personality.

We would now question the use of the concept 'personality' since put in this way it implies a self with attributes that are fixed (Gergen 1991; Pearce 1994). Harré (1980: pp. 4–5) says that 'personality' involves aspects such as our gender, the family we were brought up in, our society, culture, and religion, as well as our bodily experiences of the world and so on. It is more to do with what we *do* and *the way* we express ourselves with others in public performances and the quality of these performances *im*press other people, who express their perceptions in ways that *im*press us, and so on.

It may seem obvious to say that hypotheses must be drawn from the data, the information that the client gives us, but therapists sometimes go into realms of fantasy that bear no relation to anything overt or even implicit about the client. Hypothesising must be *thoroughly grounded* in factual information. And this process 'is a way of giving attention to the unique details of (the client) and connecting with ... (their) unique coherence' (Lang and McAdam 1995: p. 76). In the hypothesising process we 'create connections between stories, different events and different emotions... we are always building on information' (Cecchin 2002). Observing Cecchin in a workshop demonstrating hypothesising was a joy, as he made connections in an imaginative, respectful yet irreverent manner (Cecchin 2002). Our professional theories about people will of course profoundly influence the way we talk about them and with them.

As we have seen, Andy's fascination with the idea of loss, a favourite therapeutic story, attuned him to this aspect of Brenda's story.

Cecchin et al. (1992) write irreverently that therapy models are inventions created by people who are 'brilliant masters at creating elegant and useful approaches... based upon some prejudice'. In the family therapy field, they say that amongst others Selvini notices 'plots and conspiracies', Carter and McGoldrick: 'family development', Goldner or Michael White: 'oppressive patriarchies', whilst Virginia Satir's prejudice is 'love conquers all'.

In the extract below Cecchin challenges Boscolo's prejudice as they hypothesise about a family:

> Boscolo: I've noticed that frequently the son and daughter from a previous marriage has more the possibility of developing problems...
> Cecchin: ... when he makes a statement like that, I try to say something totally opposite. I'm always aware of how easy it is to make a statement like 'every time you have an adopted child, you have these problems. Every time you have a sister who is beautiful, then the other one goes crazy.' You have to be aware of this danger.
> Boscolo: ... There are infinite possibilities for the hypotheses, but some fit better than others, some connect more of the data.
> Cecchin: The hypotheses are better when they are made by therapists who are circular and who respond continuously to the feedback... (from the client) in the session. (Boscolo et al. 1987: 163)

Boscolo and Cecchin show how we can use a prejudice then discard it when it is not useful, and be able to juxtapose other prejudices to form hybrids.

Curiosity: or not falling in love with our hypotheses

Chapter 5 showed how 'curiosity' and 'self–other-reflexivity' help us to continue looking for different descriptions even when we cannot immediately imagine this possibility. And hypothesising, Cecchin (1987: 411) says, is 'what we do in order to maintain our fundamental stance of curiosity'. However, when we are very sure of the veracity of a hypothesis or a particular explanation this is extremely dangerous. 'When hypotheses ... do not help us to maintain a sense of curiosity, we have very likely stumbled upon a hypothesis that we are too willing to believe and accept (as we usually say, we "marry" our own hypotheses)' (Cecchin 1987: 412). When we 'fall in love with', or 'marry', one hypothesis we have lost our curiosity. This is a troubling sign for a systemic therapist!

We must remain constantly vigilant about information that contradicts our favourite hypothesis, so we can avoid 'falling in love' with it. Being curious when we hypothesise before, during and after conversations, means:

- staying alert to our own emotional responses;
- questioning any strong explanations;
- noticing when we take one position to the exclusion of all others.

We cannot help being moved by some clients' stories and being aware of our emotional responses to what the client tells us is vital. Lang and McAdam (1995) write 'Systemic story creation provides a way of managing your own forms of self-consciousness and emotions.' But these 'powerful emotions tend to create a uni-verse rather than a multi-verse', which means that 'you get more easily stuck in the belief that there is only one reality or story' (p. 77). 'The conceptualisation of reality as a multiverse of meanings created in dynamic social exchange and conversation interaction moves us away from concerns about issues of unique truths and into a multiverse that includes a diversity of conflicting versions of the world' say Anderson and Goolishian (1988: 378).

If I were Brenda's therapist I may notice how strongly I want to protect Brenda from her 'nasty' manager. But this may prevent me being curious about other ways of seeing things. Exploring neglected voices (such as her colleagues', friends' or family's) and asking what they would say about her relationship with her manager would expand my hypothesis.

Pearce (1989) writes, 'Whatever language is spoken around us contains in it the plot lines of a thousand tales and semantic connections between some ideas and not others.' And 'I believe that there are literally, an infinite number of stories that fit any set of facts' (p. 71). 'No matter how many stories you already have to explain why human beings are born and die you can always come up with one more' (p. 69). This is perhaps more challenging to do when we work with a client who has been abused or tortured or someone who wants to die. We can be passionate about a particular story, but these are the very times in which other voices can help us develop multiple stories and find different ways to respond. 'The more stories you have before meeting (a client) the greater the number of ways we can make sense of the stories which we are hearing and co-creating' say Lang and McAdam (1995: 96). However, it is not simply a matter of 'the more stories the merrier'; these hypotheses must make a good fit with the *details* of the client and their life, be systemic (not linear) and bring forth the client's abilities. Unfortunately, as Boscolo and Cecchin write, 'we are surprised how easily and naturally we can think of unhelpful hypotheses'. But, 'nobody changes under a negative connotation' (Boscolo 1987: p. 15).

Hypotheses must be circular and appreciative

Cecchin (1987: 412) says that 'When hypotheses stop helping us to construct circular questions . . . we have very likely stumbled upon one that we are too willing to believe and accept . . .'. In order to avoid doing this we:

- seek to understand the 'logic' of the client's (and others') meanings and actions;
- notice the significance of their relationships;
- notice similarities and differences between the client's stories and those of all the important people in their life;
- make connections between their present and past difficulties and their future dreams;
- make connections between their present difficulties, future dreams and their past stories;
- identify the client's (and others') GRRAACCCES: gender, religion, race, age, abilities, culture, class, colour, ethnic and sexual orientation stories;
- bring forth the strengths and competencies of the client and all those important people in their life;
- frame hypotheses in appreciative language.

As may be imagined, this process requires both rigour and creativity. It does not come 'naturally', even for therapists doing specific training in which they work in systemic teams, since it requires a particular kind of openness: the ability to simultaneously make multiple connections and to reject those that do not fit for the client. Continually re-evaluating and revising our hypotheses in an ongoing process throughout the therapeutic conversation as the client responds to our questions requires tremendous agility. Partly this is because we inevitably have only a limited number of personal and professional discourses on which to draw.

The Milan team develop hypothesising

The Milan team used the term 'hypothesising' as one of their three interrelated guidelines (hypothesising, circularity and neutrality). 'If "neutrality" was the basic stance and "circular questioning" the tool, "hypothesising" offered a rough scaffolding on which to hang the masses of information' (Hoffman 1981: p. 294). Hypothesising is meant to be 'a starting point for the investigation', not a statement of truth (Selvini et al. 1980: p. 4). Cecchin (in Boscolo et al. 1987: p. 163) says 'if we believe there is only one right hypothesis we go crazy trying to find it. The main thing is to experience how stuck the family is. So first we brainstorm . . . It is too easy to move to solutions if you don't have the experience of being stuck.'

The four therapists always worked in a team (usually a male and a female therapist in the room with the family and two others behind a one-way screen). This helped to prevent the therapist from getting caught up in one set of responses. Before meeting the family they would start with a number of 'linear' (causal) explanations based on whatever information was available about them, then create a provisional hypothesis, neither true nor false, but more or less useful. The therapist would then explore each idea, discard it and develop other ones as they learned more information about the family, their relationships, the evolution of their concerns and desires and so on, building up multiple explanations, systemic descriptions to 'track relational patterns' (Selvini et al. 1980). When one systemic hypothesis did not resonate or produce 'news of difference' (Bateson 1972) and therefore change, they would co-create another one, and so on until things had changed and therapy was no longer needed.

This continuous process of trial and error through asking questions helped the therapist to join the family and include all the relevant extended relationships and contexts. They aimed to produce an overarching systemic hypothesis. However, 'We could . . . work for half an hour to develop a beautiful hypothesis which included all the elements in the system . . . and then discard it in a few minutes if it revealed itself to be useless' writes Cecchin (1992: p. 90).

The five-part session, which they created, helps systemic therapists to avoid falling in love with one hypothesis, by involving others in the process of exploring hunches, observations, connections and hypotheses before, during and after each session (see Appendix 1 to this volume). 'Live supervision' (when the supervisor is behind a one-way screen or even in the same room) is a powerful way to help trainee therapists develop hypotheses during the session. Indeed Cecchin (2002) said that he always works with a colleague or a team. However, there are many ways that a therapist working alone with an individual can adapt this model by using systemic principles.

Developing hypothesising skills

Systemic hypothesising is much easier to learn with other systemic thinkers. It is akin to brainstorming: other voices making connections and contributing with ideas that generate more imaginative hypotheses. 'You need to confront your own linear thinking' Cecchin says (in Boscolo et al. 1987) 'with the linear thinking of someone else . . . (as each) tries to add something that *appears* totally unconnected, although it is of course connected in some way' (p. 165).

I was demonstrating systemic interviewing with a group of therapists who were not familiar with these ideas but I had neglected to describe the purpose and process of hypothesising. Dawn volunteered to be interviewed, and role-played a 39-year-old female client. She said (in role) that she had come to therapy because her boyfriend had recently ended their relationship. She had had several broken relationships and called this 'a pattern'. I drew a genogram/family tree with her help and noticed that she was the only unmarried sibling, and was closest to her mother and began to develop one hypothesis that perhaps she was keeping herself free (for the time being) for this stronger relationship. One of the things I was curious about was whether she chose men who were not 'free' themselves, or did not want a long-term relationship. However, I had not 'married' my hypothesis, so I turned to the group for help.

Being used to working with systemic colleagues I expected a joyous brainstorming of ideas that connected with and extended my developing hypothesis. I hoped that they would have noticed her language, my responses and what we were co-creating together through our verbal and non-verbal communication. I expected them to build on these observations in a respectful, yet playful and creative way, developing multivariously rich, sometimes contradictory, stories. Suddenly someone said 'But, it's obvious; she's upset because her relationship has ended.'

At the time I was silenced by the general consensus that this was the end of the story. In retrospect I realise that I could have used the opportunity to explain hypothesising and taken this idea as a starting point. I could have said 'Now let's create some stories (hypotheses) about how she decided to come to talk now.' 'What do you think most upset her about the relationship ending?' 'Who else was upset that the relationship had ended? Or conversely, 'Who do you think might be pleased or even relieved that the relationship had ended?' In this way we could have begun to make systemic connections with significant others in her life, identified our prejudices and begun to question them.

Hypothesising when working alone

Unaccompanied therapists can adapt the five-stage model when they work with an individual by using reported supervision before and between each conversation. It is useful to make an audiotape or videotape of the conversation to review afterwards and/or with a supervisor or colleague.

Between sessions we can:

- do a 'mindmap' immediately after the session;
- write verbatim notes of the session, articulate and reflect on our hypotheses;
- ask colleagues what hypotheses they think we have been using;
- attend workshops about difference;
- read widely, literature and biographies as well as theory/practice texts;
- have conversations with people from a different culture, class, gender or religious background and so on to our own;
- watch other systemic therapists at work;
- see films, theatre plays and television plays and documentaries about people who live different lives from our own.

During the conversations we can explore our hypotheses by:

- asking circular (relationship) questions to bring in other voices from the client's life;
- asking the client what ideas and theories *they* think we are using;
- oscillating between observer and therapy positions during the session;
- taking a short break away from the client to talk with an imaginary other;
- deliberately turning a story on its head to create an opposite hypothesis.

In order to question my 'favourite story' that Dawn's 'disastrous' choice of partners is related in some way to the idea that she is showing loyalty to her relationship with her mother, I can ask 'Whom did you first tell when Tim told you the relationship was over?' If she says 'I rang my mum right away' this would verify one aspect of the hypothesis. But I would not accept this as 'proven', and would continue to explore this idea by asking further circular questions such as 'How did she respond?' Then (depending on her answer) 'What did you say/do then?' and so on and on to build up a picture of these feedback loops. I could also ask her what ideas she thinks are guiding my questions and responses.

We can turn a story on its head. It is 'better to have two competing hypotheses, then you can see if they confirm each other' (Cecchin in Boscolo et al. 1987: p. 166).

I might hypothesise that Dawn had not told anybody about the split because she was protecting somebody from her sadness. Or on the other hand she could be protecting herself, from possible derogatory remarks about her ex and the unsuitability of the relationship. Or maybe this is how she typically responds, or maybe she is trying something different. I could ask 'What made you decide to keep it to yourself?' If she says 'Because I didn't want to upset anybody', I could ask 'If you were able to tell somebody, who would it be?' She may answer that she would like to tell both her parents but did not want to bother them 'because they were already upset about my sister'. This gives us valuable information about the family. I might hypothesise that she had decided to be the 'good daughter'.

As the client responds to the questions we ask they will inevitably give us new information that modifies, extends or disproves our hypothesis. In this way we will form a second, third and even fourth hypothesis, until enough change has taken place for therapy not to be necessary.

Perhaps, taking a different tack altogether, I might notice that Dawn is 39 and wonder if she (or others in her family or peer-group) believes that time is running out for her to have children. I may be curious about whether there is a connection between her distress at the ending of the relationship and stories about procreation. Parents can wish for a grandchild. This is seen as sign of 'success' in many cultures (including our own). A woman may refer to her 'body clock' whilst a man has much longer to decide whether to have children. There may be a class story that links with family and professional stories and children and her age.

We could wonder if her career was her passport out of the prescribed future of becoming a wife and mother. Maybe Dawn had been struggling with a dilemma about whether to do further professional training or have a child?

In this way we constantly extend our range of ideas and stories, become more creative and curious, making *systemic* connections. And this enables us to avoid reaching for favourite explanations (as Boscolo did above), automatically noticing a 'familiar pattern', or becoming very sure that we know what is going on. 'The more stories you have before meeting (a client) the greater the number of ways we can make sense of the stories which we are hearing and co-creating' say Lang and McAdam (1995: 96).

Hypothesising from the outset

We make connections the moment we hear about a client. If we are able to speak to a person when they make an appointment, their tone of voice and accent, as well as what they say, will connect us to various stories and ideas that may or may not be 'accurate'.

The phone rings, a young woman with a hesitant voice asks 'Can I, er, I'd like to, er, can I, er, can I talk to somebody?' Everything about her words and tone makes me think she is unused to this context. But this may not be the case.

When we meet the client we will develop ideas based on their gender, physical appearance, colour, clothes, hair, demeanour, gestures and so on even before we hear their words. When they speak their voice, accent, tone and pace will give us further information.

A tall black woman in her late 20s strides into a therapy centre reception and says 'I've come to arrange counselling.' The word 'arrange' and the way she says it make me wonder if she has done this before.

A white man in his mid 30s comes to meet me for the first time. I notice his hesitant smile, his slight build, casual clothes, earring, closely shaven head, unshaven face (some call this 'designer stubble'). Maybe he is in some branch of the creative arts? The way he perches on the edge of the chair makes me think he is a bit nervous.

We create stories about a person based on even small amounts of information. Pearce (1989: p. 69) writes, 'None of us is thrown completely on our own resources to make the world coherent.' Experience of previous clients, professional stories from colleagues or stories from our own personal experiences, stories told in our community or culture, stories from literature, cinema and the theatre also create our hypotheses. In some contexts we will know something about a client before we meet them.

I receive a referral letter from a GP who writes 'Ms Sunita Patel is suffering from depression.' I immediately wonder if she could be sleeping a lot, or not sleeping very much or if she is neglecting her physical needs. She could have financial problems that are making her 'depressed': she may be unemployed, having a struggle to keep her job. Maybe Sunita is taking 'time out' to contemplate her next step in life? Any number of things may have affected the referral to me.

The contexts in which we work are extremely important. I wonder what brought her to the surgery and what she communicated to the doctor so that he came to refer her to me. I may know that this particular GP uses the term 'depression' very loosely. Maybe Sunita has enlisted the GP (a respected authority figure) to witness her distress about something important?

Sunita is 18 and my ideas about the needs, expectations and tasks of an 18-year-old woman living in Britain will affect how I respond. Her Asian name makes me wonder whether her parents came from another culture whilst she was brought up in Britain. Does she have dilemmas about identity? I am reminded of recent news stories about arranged and enforced marriages. If Sunita says that indeed her parents have begun to choose a husband for her, I may leap to the cliché that she wants to marry for love, rather than accept her parents' wishes to have a hand in choosing her husband.

Before I even meet Sunita I will have many hypotheses to work with based on very little information: some may fit, others may immediately become irrelevant. In practice we 'usually begin with a linear causal statement about one or two people' Boscolo et al. (1987: p. 170) write. Exploring one or two ideas gives direction and focus to the work. As we have seen, just by focusing on the description 'depressed', Sunita's age and her name we still have a rich vein of stories to explore.

In order to create some useful hypotheses I could ask Sunita:

- What did she say/do to the GP so that he described her as 'depressed' (and referred her for talking therapy)?
- To whom does she 'show' 'depression'?
- When (in which contexts) does she feel sad/low/miserable?
- What does she *do* that makes people describe her as 'depressed'?
- For how long has she acted in these ways?
- Who has noticed?
- What are other people's hopes, wishes and dreams for her future?
- What sense does she make of her own behaviour, thoughts and feelings?
- What stories are being told about her in the family, with her friends, in her community?
- What are Sunita's own hopes, dreams and wishes for the future?

Our systemic stories may initially be rather simple, then rather like a jazz player improvising on a riff, we can develop the themes until they become more complex systemic stories.

Jake was a young homeless man living in a night shelter who talked about the guilt that he felt towards his mother about 'running away' from Scotland. I began to hypothesise on the theme of running away; was that something young men in his family/community did? Or was he unusual? I wondered about guilt and his relationship with his mother. We explored the meaning of running away and I learned about his difficult relationship with his father.

I turned this idea upside down, wondering aloud what was he running towards? He became animated and talked about opportunities 'down South' that he had always dreamed of.

Rather than using an either-or, I worked with a both-and perspective.

Using the running away/running towards themes connected us with frustrations and dilemmas experienced by men such as his father who lived in a small fishing community. Jake began to describe himself as both an adventurer and a loyal son. This was a pivotal moment for both of us in the work.

Systemic hypothesising with an individual

Before the first session the therapist

- has a conversation with a supervisor or colleague if possible;
- notices their own reactions to any information about the client;
- considers who may be included in the 'system in focus';
- develops ideas, stories and a provisional systemic hypothesis;
- prepares circular questions to check out their hypotheses.

During the conversation the therapist

- tapes the session so that they can review the details of the conversation;
- follows an idea or hypothesis by asking circular questions;
- explores communications between people in the client's life;
- follows the client's grammar and language;
- notices the effect of their own stories on the conversation;
- abandons an idea/hypothesis as soon as it does not fit for the client;
- explores a new idea and story to create a new hypothesis;
- turns their hypothesis upside down or finds an opposite hypothesis;
- asks the client what they think of the therapist's ideas;
- notices when strong emotions make them 'fall in love' with their hypothesis;
- notices if there is a strong story that obliterates all others;
- constantly reflects on the effect of their language (gestures, attitudes, expressions) on the client;
- asks the client at the end of the conversation if they have developed any new ideas or new connections.

Other ways to develop new hypotheses during the session

- Take a short break away from the client to connect to new ideas.
- 'Ask Teddy' – imagine an unusual but wise onlooker who offers a new or even a naïve perspective.

Immediately after each session the therapist

- makes brief notes (and/or draws a mindmap);
- writes verbatim notes;
- reviews which of their hypotheses are now redundant;
- creates new hypotheses for the following session;
- reflects on the effect of their ideas and feelings on the client;
- reviews questions/responses that have been most/least useful;
- considers what they are still puzzled about;
- celebrates their work.

Between sessions the therapist

- reviews their work by listening to the audiotape or viewing a videotape;
- writes verbatim notes of a section of the conversation;
- explores their hypotheses in supervision and/or with colleagues;
- reflects on the way their ideas and hypotheses have shaped the conversation;
- reflects on how their attitude/behaviour shaped the conversation;
- reflects on how the client responded to their ideas and questions.

In developing hypotheses or systemic stories the therapist

- is always curious (not certain);
- sees the client as the expert in their life;
- works with the connections and communications between the client and the important others in their life (not an individual in isolation);
- tries to make sense of everyone's actions;
- is appreciative of the position of everybody involved;
- sees that everyone is doing their best given all the circumstances;
- uses the verb 'to show' (not the verb 'to be');
- makes connections between present difficulties, future dreams and past stories;
- closely follows the client's language;
- works creatively with the client's language;
- is open to multiple (even contradictory) ways of describing things;
- notices how their language and their hypotheses affect the client;
- discards favourite ideas as soon as they do not 'fit' or resonate for the client;
- asks questions to explore their hypothesis/systemic story;
- is alert to relevant political, societal and gender stories;
- is alert to relevant race, culture, ethnic and colour stories;
- is alert to relevant religious and ethical stories;
- is alert to relevant family and personal identity stories;
- is alert to stories related to age, size and so on;
- is alert to their own relevant professional stories;
- has conversations with colleagues from different cultural, race, colour, gender and class backgrounds;
- reads widely, sees films, plays and so on about people who are very different from ourselves.

A systemic hypothesis

- is based on *what the client tells us* (verbally and non-verbally) about themselves and others;
- includes the voices of important others in their life (as well as any referrers);
- makes connections between important people in the client's life;
- positively connotes all their important relationships;
- positively connotes the 'symptoms' for example, if a person is making themselves sick, how is this sometimes useful?;
- makes connections between events in the client's life;
- works with past, present and future;
- has *at least* two opposing ideas;
- involves multiple descriptions;
- includes the concept of time;
- takes into account what is being co-created between therapist and client;
- is seen simply as a temporary explanation/description;
- avoids linear, causal and individualistic explanations.

8
FUTURE DREAMING AND APPRECIATING ABILITIES

The future influences more the way... we live in the present than anything that happened in the past
                                          Lang and McAdam (1997)

Imagination is more important than knowledge
                                                    Albert Einstein

Just one idea or image can transform the entire gestalt of a thousand others
                                                 Cooperrider (1990)

When some therapists hear that we can co-create more effective change by (1) working more with the future than the past and (2) appreciating clients' abilities rather than their deficits, they dismiss these ideas as self-evident and even banal. But their work shows that they have not understood the importance of doing this. These practices are immensely powerful in encouraging optimism in clients and therapists alike, but they are not easy to use because they often go against what feels 'natural', that is, the urge to explore clients' problems. When I first began to use these ways of working it was a privilege to witness the almost immediate energising effect on both my clients and my own stories. And these approaches continue to help me honour colleagues, clients, my organisation, and myself, so I feel more optimistic about the future. This chapter aims to demonstrate how to put these concepts into practice.

Firstly, in order to make a contrast, I will show a systemic therapist working respectfully with a client's narrative and his significant relationships, but not with the client's abilities or his future dreams.

Scenario 1

The therapist warmly greets Trevor, a man in his early 50s, who has come to talk for the first time in his life. Trevor says that he has been working at a small printing company for 15 years as a supervising printer, but he has been on sick leave for some months, 'confused' and scared that he is 'losing his mind'. Exploring these fears Trevor tells the therapist that he has enormous financial problems. His boss values him but thinks he is 'having a breakdown'. Trevor's wife Rose does not know the extent of the problems and this is inadvertently creating conflict as Rose is 'nagging' him for going 'moody'. Trevor hates any kind of confrontation. The therapist respectfully works to understand how these difficulties have developed over the years: he and Rose come from impoverished backgrounds. Rose wants a different life and Trevor wants to help her make her dreams come true. He describes himself as 'weak' in the face of her desire for material possessions. He has withdrawn from his two grown-up children, colleagues and life itself. Now he says he is 'living a lie': well regarded at work, but out of control with money.

Of course, this example is greatly simplified in order to make the point, and there are many ways in which this therapist *is* helping Trevor. However, if the therapist were to tap into his abilities and potentials they could co-create positive emotions, optimism and change in a much briefer time frame.

In this chapter I describe the following energising practices:

- hypothetical future questions (Boscolo et al. 1987; Penn 1984);
- 'appreciative inquiry' (Cooperrider 1990).

Lang and McAdam (1997) build on 'hypothetical future questions' (variations on circular questions), which, they say, helped them 'see a future in which the intractable, the puzzling, the so-called chaotic ... might be processes of ... change' (3). They draw on Dewey's metaphor of the future shaping the present (in Tiles 1988), and Wittgenstein's (1953) concept of 'emergent rule games' to enhance their work, through:

- 'ability-spotting';
- 'dream talk'.

A future approach

The Milan team (Selvini et al. 1980) note that our society is permeated with ideas about causality: we tend to see difficulties in the present as being *caused by* things that happened in the past. However, Boscolo et al. (1987: p. 134) write 'When you ask about the future you can't be deterministic.' The Milan team had created the 'positive/logical connotation', a powerful way of not blaming clients or their symptoms. Later Boscolo and Cecchin (known as the post-Milan team) developed 'hypothetical future questions'. These questions 'challenge a (client's) . . . premise or advance a new one (and) . . . evoke a different map'. Clients, writes Tomm (1987: 173) 'are sometimes so preoccupied with present difficulties or past injustices that . . . they live as if they "have no future" . . . they remain impoverished with respect to future alternatives and choices'. Future questions allow clients to construct possible future worlds (Boscolo and Bertrando 1996: p. 172), and these questions, Lang and McAdam (1997: 3) say, 'created the greatest possibilities for change than any work that looked at the past'.

Consider the following alternative scenario of the first meeting with Trevor.

Scenario 2

After warmly greeting Trevor the therapist asks 'What are you hoping for from this conversation?' Trevor says that he's been very confused of late and would like to be less so.

This question immediately identifies what Trevor wants from the conversation. 'From the very beginning . . . we abandon the neutrality of "What would you like to talk about?" . . . Instead we talk immediately about hopes . . . for this particular therapeutic conversation . . . for the whole process of therapy' (Lang and McAdam 1997: 8).

The therapist says 'less confused?' using Trevor's language. 'Perhaps a bit clearer?' she adds. Trevor agrees.

This introduces the idea of 'clarity'. 'An optimistic consultant creates possibilities; a pessimistic consultant creates chronic difficulties and intractable problems for the people with whom he is working' says Lang (2003).

The therapist could ask Trevor about his hopes for the whole process of therapy now. But if he is highly distressed or prefers to talk right away about his difficulties, she could ask the following questions (and explore the answers) at the end of the conversation: 'Imagine that therapy had been successful, what would you notice about yourself?' 'What would other people notice about you? What would you be doing differently?' and

'Imagine that therapy had made your hopes and dreams seem more possible, what do you imagine doing differently?' (Hedges 2000).

Our view of the future is in the here and now creating and *informing the present* say Lang and McAdam (1997: 5–6) drawing on Dewey's notion that 'the end' forms the present, and does not simply reside in the future (in Tiles 1988: p. 195).

Trevor says that he is afraid to 'confess' his debts to his wife Rose and is ashamed that people will find out. His confusion relates to not knowing how to move forward.

Dewey uses two metaphors. The first is of an archer, aiming at a target at the end of a field. Every decision that the archer makes about how to stand, how to hold the arrow and the bow is formed by the future hope that the arrow will hit the bull's eye. Similarly, he says, when we build a house, first there is the image of the house. This informs each stage of the building process, the materials used and the meaning of every action. The present is imbued with ('points towards') the future. If all our actions in the present are done with an 'end in view', this is very different from focusing on how problems were created in the past. Doing this takes great skill, and often feels 'unnatural'.

Trevor's vision of the future, his 'end in view', involves fearful images of destitution.

But the future is 'permeable, emergent . . . reality is conditioned, reconstructed, and often profoundly created through our anticipatory images, values, plans, intentions, beliefs, and the like' says Cooperrider (1990: p. 52).

'What kind of future do you long for?' the therapist asks. Trevor talks about his desire for a comfortable retirement. The two scenarios do not fit but now the therapist can explore ways to help Trevor create the more hopeful one.

'People need to be affirmed; they don't need problem analysis but affirmation. When I see repetitive patterns that are destructive I go into the future' says Cooperrider (1996). However, Lang and McAdam (1997: 8) say that to ignore clients' problems could be disrespectful. Indeed problems could be 'examples of frustrated hopes and dreams' (Lang and McAdam 1997).

Trevor talks about his financial difficulties, his withdrawal from his family, and inability to go to work. The therapist, following his language, asks questions to make connections and understand.

We explore the kind of future our client wishes for and how their problems could be preventing this. 'These future oriented discussions create 'a "by pass" around the negativity of problem voices' write Lang and McAdam (1997: 8). However, we do not insist on this focus, otherwise we 'create a tyranny' says Lang (2003). We respect and negotiate ways that fit best for the client and are sensitive to their timing.

Trevor wants to be back at work, clear-headed and functioning well. In the ideal world he would have sorted out his finances and by some miracle he and Rose would have found a way of working cooperatively on these tricky issues. In fact he would have returned to the 'old happy-go-lucky Trevor'.

Another word of caution: although working optimistically with the future is powerful, when we simply visualise a good future this can show the past as deficient (Cooperrider 1990). It is crucial to also draw on 'the best of what is', and 'the best of what has been', and include resources that otherwise have been missed.

The therapist explores the times and contexts in which Trevor functions well. She learns how he is valued at work. He talks about a time when he and his wife pulled together. As he notices these resources he begins to envision a time when he could build on them in the future. These hopeful images create optimistic emotions. He leans back in the chair and begins to smile (perhaps ruefully at this stage).

By changing the language that people use we develop 'a change in the emotions and emotionality' (Lang and McAdam 1997: 8). 'Images of hope and hopefulness can affect the body's innate healing system, its immune functioning, and other neurochemical processes' writes Cooperrider (in Srivastva and Cooperrider 1990: p. 108). And, when we notice that clients change in positive ways, we feel energised and joyful.

Hypothetical future questions

Hypothetical questions are 'what if?' questions and get clients thinking creatively, making different connections and envisioning different scenarios.

Trevor can never tell anybody about his debts. 'If you were able to talk to somebody (apart from me) who would it be?' the therapist asks. 'Perhaps I could tell Rose... give her a hint about things... see what she says' he replies. The therapist notes that Trevor sees himself as a potential negotiator.

When clients show that they are beginning to consider new ways of acting this always gives me hope. 'Hypothetical questions' says Penn (1984: 300) 'enable the person to create a new map and give the client a sense of their own potential'.

'I wonder what you would need to do to prepare for that conversation?' the therapist asks, helping Trevor to try out different contexts.

Future questions illuminate the present. 'When you consider your own condition in the future you are automatically fitting another context around your present context' writes Penn (1984: 301).

He has always taken sole financial responsibility for the family: he and Rose are 'home-loving'; she enjoys spending her earnings (described as 'pin-money') on their beautiful home. They have evolved a way of dealing with money: his earnings pay for the 'real things' (mortgage and bills), whilst Rose's earnings are seen as her own. The therapist explores Rose's enjoyment of home-making and learns that she is making up for a tough childhood. 'Perhaps you've been helping her make her dreams come true?' the therapist asks. Trevor likes this idea. He smiles broadly.

The therapist does not explore Rose's past 'difficulties', their 'lack of communication' or any other pejorative descriptions, but shows appreciation of the logic of both their actions. She bases this on the idea that they are both doing the best they can, given all the circumstances.

Other hypothetical questions explore how they deal with money.

'If you and Rose hadn't organised your finances as you have done would you be closer to her or less close now?' Trevor does not know, but it resonates for him and later he says they would be closer if had they shared financial decisions.

'Imagine that you and Rose had spent your money on other things what might your life look like now?'

'Well, we're both stay-at homes, so we wouldn't have such a comfortable house' he laughs. 'And if Rose hadn't been able to buy those things she wouldn't have been so happy. And I want Rose to be happy.'

Previously he did not know where the money had gone. Now he is clearer. Now he says there *was* some logic; they spent money on creating a beautiful home. As Harré (2001) says 'What people do in the future is based on what they *think* they did in the past.' Trevor had previously believed that he was a failure at managing money and unable to curb his wife's overspending. Now he uses a different metaphor: they had been 'building a home together'. This is an exciting moment for both Trevor and the therapist. Trevor and Rose *have* worked as a competent team so can do this again in the future.

Building on this metaphor the therapist asks 'By creating a home together, working as a team, how would it be if you continue to protect Rose from the reality of your debts?'

The word 'protect' does two things: (1) since Trevor feels 'bad enough', it offers a more positive connotation and (2) it projects Trevor into the future. 'Questions about the future, in conjunction with positive connotation, put (clients) . . . in a meta position to their own dilemmas and thus facilitate change by opening up new solutions for old problems' (Penn 1984: 229).

Trevor replies, 'They might repossess the house.' He looks worried.

Although the possibility of losing the house is shocking, the therapist hears Trevor, perhaps for the first time, articulating his worst nightmare. The word 'reality' has got him considering how the future *could be* if he and Rose persist in this way of living. These questions allow 'the discussion of a forbidden topic and (provide) a safe and indirect way of answering a question that could not be posed directly' (Boscolo et al. 1987: p. 257).

Now, permitted to explore this possibility, the therapist asks 'Imagine that you had found a way to keep the house?' 'We might have to face up to what's going on,' Trevor replies.

Although he fears confrontation with Rose, he is considering involving her in their finances; this can be an exciting moment for a therapist. 'Future-oriented questions . . . can be used to stimulate a (client) . . . to entertain possibilities that they may never have considered on their own, yet are compatible with the pre-existing values and beliefs' writes Tomm (1987: 174).

'And what if you had found a way to help her to understand?' the therapist asks. *'I could tell her how bad things have got'* Trevor replies. *'And how might she respond?'* He looks alarmed. *'What if she's angry? She might be shocked. She might cry.'* *'What if she's relieved?'* the therapist adds offering an alternative scenario. *'She'd probably say "why didn't you tell me?"* Trevor says then adds quietly *'Maybe she'd think about what she's buying.'*

The therapist does not want Trevor to think that this is the best (or only) way of moving into a better future since it could negatively connote Rose.

'As well as that, what other things could you imagine both of you doing to help you to save the house?' the therapist asks.

This opens space for Trevor to explore creative alternatives and shows that whilst their joint actions in the past (their earning and spending habits) and their individual identity stories may have led to their current difficulties, there could be other ways of moving forward.

However, Trevor says he 'doesn't know', since 'we've always done things the same way'.

'The world we have made . . . creates problems we cannot solve at the same level of thinking at which we created them,' says Einstein, (quoted in Lang and McAdam 1997: 8).

'What if you did know?' the therapist asks.

This question is extremely helpful when a client replies 'I don't know'; it usually connects them to information that they actually do have but may not have considered.

'Maybe we'd work out some better ways to manage our money' he says.

'Where did you develop your ways of money management?' the therapist asks. Now Trevor talks about how his father always took control of the family's finances and how he and Rose have followed suit.

'If a family is organized around a premise that is creating a problem, future questions can ... challenge the power of the premise to continue into the future' write Boscolo et al. (1987: p. 34). Trevor's (and Rose's) 'premises' seem to involve: 'a real man always manages the family's finances' and 'the man's, not the woman's, earnings are counted as real income.'

The therapist explores other family members' financial arrangements. Trevor says that his son and daughter both pool their money and discuss finances with their partners. 'Which method would you prefer if you had a fresh start?' This links Trevor to a hypothetical future in which he could take some different action.

'These questions', Boscolo et al. (1987: p. 203 write, 'create connections; they reveal myths, self-fulfilling prophecies, and expectations which ... are usually not talked about'.

Trevor considers the pros and cons of each approach. 'Rose and I might work things out our own way.'

Trevor's new use of the pronouns 'we' and 'our' in place of the earlier use of 'I', 'me', 'my, and 'she' is extremely fascinating. We could hypothesise that he now positions himself less as an isolated bearer of the family's financial 'burdens', and more as someone in a mutually supportive relationship.

Feeling a little elated the therapist muses 'I wonder what your (and Rose's) own way could be like?' Trevor is unsure at present but he shows, through his more erect body posture, his smile, and his lighter and more hopeful tone of voice that he is beginning to feel more optimistic.

When I notice these bodily changes in a client I begin to feel exhilarated. 'Questions about the future have enormous impact on the non-verbal behaviours' Boscolo et al. (1987: pp. 134–5) write, 'You see much stronger responses to questions about the future than to questions about the past or the present.'

The therapist now risks a humorous and provocative hypothetical question. 'What if Rose were to take over the finances entirely?' Trevor laughs at this absurd idea, but shows that the solidity of his original premise has already begun to weaken.

Next time they meet Trevor surprisingly tells the therapist that he had taken 'his courage in his hands' and 'confessed' to his son Gerry about his financial difficulties. Gerry had been shocked but supportive. This eventually made it easier to tell Rose, who was relieved to understand his withdrawal. Together they began the complicated process of negotiating with the financial bodies. A new closeness developed between them all.

Appreciative inquiry

The questions we ask determine what we find. What we focus on expands. Some people misunderstand an appreciative approach to be a Pollyanna-like dichotomy between 'being positive' and 'being negative'. But a much subtler both/and process is involved. Cooperrider and Srivastva's (1990) Appreciative Inquiry approach in organisations has inspired systemic therapists to shift from exploring how problems have been created in the past to envisioning possible futures. At the same time we identify what is life-affirming in the present and what has been life-affirming in the past.

Cooperrider (1990) draws from four distinct areas of research to underpin this approach, which I outline in what follows:

(1) positive imagery, medicine and the placebo;
(2) Pygmalion and the positive construction of the Other;
(3) positive affect and learned helpfulness;
(4) the off-balance internal dialogue.

Positive imagery, medicine and the placebo

The medical profession now accepts the efficacy of the placebo effect says Cooperrider (1990): 'positive changes in anticipatory reality through suggestion and belief play a central role in all placebo responses' and 'positive imagery can and often does awaken the body to its own self-healing powers' (p. 99). 'The power of positive imagery is not just some popular illusion or wish but is arguably a key factor in every action' he says (Cooperrider 1990: p. 99). In sports research, two groups learning to play bowls were filmed on video. In one group everything except the person's failures was erased. In the second group everything except their successes was erased. Three months later although both groups had improved, the positive feedback group had improved twice as much as the negative feedback group, a difference of 100 per cent.

If we look back at the therapist's conversation with Trevor, he began to feel better about himself when he noticed what he had already been doing well in his life (rather than focusing on how he had 'messed things up'). And his physical responses showed this.

All bodily expressions are aspects of language, says Anderson (1991). He quotes Wittgenstein (1953): 'we are *in* language and being in language we are in activity . . . all our movements also are "talking" in the sense that they are informing.'

Trevor's subtle physical changes, the slower, calmer breathing, more alert posture, fractionally faster speech and more tranquil facial expression, showed the therapist that Trevor was thinking differently and feeling better.

If I were Trevor's therapist I would feel that my work was having some positive effect and would begin to feel energised.

Pygmalion and the positive construction of the Other

Cooperrider (1987) summarises the numerous 'Pygmalion' studies that show self-fulfilling prophecy at work in the classroom. Teachers were told that some pupils (chosen at random) were brighter than others were and this created a 'positive construction' in which they actually did perform better than their peers did.

The therapist notices Trevor's resources and his competencies and he in turn begins to talk, think and act as a competent man.

Positive affect and learned helpfulness

Cooperrider (1990) shows the connection between positive emotion and learned social helpfulness. Numerous studies, he says, show that feeling, thinking and action fit together to 'create feedback loops of amplifying intensity' (pp. 105–7).

As he began to feel much better Trevor began to tackle practical tasks around the house, and he changed his self-description to that of a person who acted with the best of intentions.

Good feelings are shown to increase a person's capacity for making more effective decisions, creative problems solving, and ability to learn says Cooperrider (1990: p. 106).

Feeling good about his abilities enabled Trevor to create a more positive story about himself (and the marriage) and he felt more confident about tackling larger problems.

The off-balance internal dialogue

We are involved in an off-balance internal dialogue says Cooperrider (1990). Most of us carry many personal and professional self-blaming narratives that take time to challenge. Little wonder when, as he writes 'disturbing reports show that many of our children today are growing up in family settings where as much as 90 percent of the home's internal dialogue is negative' (p. 108). Cooperrider says that this helped him with the negative language he used with his own children, for example instead of saying 'don't do that, you'll poke your eye out', saying 'hold the stick firmly and everyone will be safe' creates quite a different scenario.

As we have noted, before Trevor came to therapy, he was bathed in an aural landscape of negative self-descriptions. The therapist spent time deconstructing them and respectfully noting any discrepancies.

Cooperrider (1990) says that our 'self-talk' or 'inner dialogue', and ongoing 'inner newsreel' powerfully affect our physiology at a neurochemical level (p. 102).

Trevor has spent a lifetime perfecting his self-blaming self-talk, so the process of bringing forth skills, resources and competencies may take time.

Blaming discourses also abound at a societal level say Srivastva and Cooperrider (1990). Notice the proliferation of blaming discourses in the media. Many therapists employ phrases such as 'low self-esteem' that describe people in terms of their deficiencies and Gergen (1991) says that we are bombarded by such descriptions, in a 'spiralling cycle of deficit terminology' that 'discredits the individual drawing attention to problems, shortcomings, or incapacities'. Created, he says, initially by 'psychiatrists and psychologists to try to explain undesirable behaviour (this language) is slowly disseminated to the public at large so that they too can become conscious of mental-health issues' (pp. 13–15). To his list of 22 'syndromes' I have recently heard about the following three:

- 'hurried woman syndrome' which affects a busy professional woman with children;
- 'Atlas syndrome' which affects men who try to be perfect at work and at home, then become depressed. Apparently the men are catching up on women who get depressed when they try to 'do it all' and 'have it all';
- 'celebrity worship syndrome' which is self-explanatory.

Like many of us, I am familiar with self-talk that reiterates my failings, and changing these stories is an ongoing process.

Trevor had previously been afraid that he was 'going mad' or 'having a breakdown' because he was so 'weak'. But his internal dialogue began to alter when the therapist helped him notice his capabilities.

However, an appreciative approach is not like a 'visioning process' in which people are encouraged to 'forget the past' says Cooperrider (1990). By simply visualising a better future this could describe the past as defective and therefore miss the 'good, true and beautiful' stories from the person's past and present life.

Ability-spotting

'Ability-spotting' goes some way to rectifying this, by appreciating 'the best of what is and what has been' (Lang and McAdam 1997). At a workshop Lang (2003) asked for a volunteer to describe their journey that morning. He then helped her to identify the complexity of skills and abilities that she had used in driving there. She began to identify abilities that she had previously taken for granted. When professionals experience the sense of joyfulness this can give us we appreciate the power this can have for our clients.

The shame of debt has been telling Trevor a story of being unworthy as a man, a husband, a son and a father. And this overshadowed the many skills he had. The therapist and Trevor then worked together to 'spot' his abilities: firstly his ability to talk openly with the therapist (unusual for a man of his age and class) and to maintain the loyalty of friends, family and colleagues. The therapist reiterates his abilities as a 'can-do' person at work, which had been spotted by colleagues and his manager. Later, Trevor himself noticed his ability to talk openly to his son and show his vulnerability.

It is stimulating as a therapist to be part of this kind of conversation, to hear a client spot their (and others') skills and abilities and resources. And these never-before-noticed abilities become part of the person's identity, says Lang (2003).

Trevor now recalls how he learned how to be a good father, husband and family man from his father. He had hitherto not noticed the invaluable lessons he had learned from both parents. They worked hard, saved for luxuries and were prudent. He now recognises how he has neglected to practise these skills for some years. Trevor now rails against large corporations that encourage debt; he does not describe himself as 'weak and incompetent' as before (although he takes responsibility for briefly joining a consumerist society).

Political and societal discourses had affected Trevor's personal identity and family stories.

Dream-talk

Problems 'may provide a focus for . . . dreaming conversations' say Lang and McAdam (1997: 8). When they asked a young woman (with shaved head and tattoos) who had been sexually abused, about her dreams, she says, somewhat surprisingly, that she longs to be a princess. Connecting with other princesses and exploring the numerous meanings of being a princess helps her to envision a future in which she is taking care of herself and acting differently with new groups of people (7).

When Trevor explores his dreams, he realises that his fear of talking to Rose about their financial problems has been frustrating his (and her) long-term dreams for a peaceful retirement. If they cannot talk about anything important, how can they sort out the major obstacle to their future dreams?

'The way the problem is defined gives some clue of the themes around which the dreaming conversations need to focus' say Lang and McAdam (1997: 8).

He and Rose are unable to communicate about money, Trevor says. Whilst they have an implicit agreement that in a few years' time they will retire to live near their daughter in the West Country, because they have never had an explicit conversation, there are potential misunderstandings. And being unable to discuss practical issues could scupper their dreams.

Working with dreams is not like creating 'goals' which imply steps, action plans and the like. 'We are not interested in being realistic' Lang and McAdam (1997: 7) say, 'only in tuning into the creative grammars that dreaming conversations will bring forth'. 'Dreams' allow mutability and flexibility. And there is a great deal more power and energy in the Martin Luther King 'I have a dream' speech than if he had said 'I have a goal' (Lang 2003).

However, Trevor's dreams remain within the bounds of possibility: he sees Rose as more involved with their grandchildren whilst he works part-time. But they are not set in stone. Perhaps they will take more foreign holidays, perhaps he will learn cabinet-making.

'Dream-talk' takes us into an 'emergent language game'. Wittgenstein contrasts this with his best-known analogy of a 'fixed rule language game' (1953: no. 197). Chess, for example, has only a certain number of 'moves' and playing the game reinforces them. In some contexts such as formal meetings, funerals and weddings ceremonies there are only a certain number of appropriate responses and by participating we reproduce them. Standing on one's head, or shouting 'Down with apple strudel' at a funeral would make people doubt one's sanity.

Trevor and Rose talk and act in a way that appears to be like a 'fixed rule language game'. There seem to be only a limited number of 'moves' with each responding in predictable ways.

Many clients with intractable problems think that nothing can change. There seems to be no possibility for something different. However, with human interaction there are *always* possibilities for new 'rules' to emerge says Wittgenstein (1953: no. 36). Everyday ordinary communication often fluctuates and this means that new 'rules' can be created. Bruner's

(1974/75) example of a mother and a young baby coordinating their actions and playing 'peek-a-boo' shows that together they develop a coordinated way of responding to each other (in Cronen and Lang 1994: 25–7). The baby hides behind something then when the baby peeks out the mother says 'boo'. 'We would say that the rules are emergent in the game' since the rule that you say 'boo' and then hide your head comes into being only in the doing of this activity (25).

'Dreaming conversations are a way of living in the world of the imagined' say Lang and McAdam (1997: 7) and the person begins to develop abilities so that they can 'walk into an attainable dream'.

Previously any deviation from the way Trevor and Rose had managed the family's finances would have felt 'unnatural'. But at the next session Trevor says that somehow he got the glimmer of a new idea (to talk to his son).

Visualising a future in which he is drawing on his existing abilities gives Trevor a glimpse of how the future could be and how he could get there. When this happens in a session this can be a joyful moment. Lang and McAdam (1997) describe working with a young person referred by a school for persistent stealing. They did *not* work with the language of helping the young person to 'stop stealing', since 'stop' keeps the negative imagery of 'theft' alive. But working on his dreams brought out his hopes of getting on well at school, having friends, and being safe. This led to ways in which he was doing this already. Therapists sometimes have to search for tiny ways in which a person shows skills, abilities and resources.

Earlier, it had seemed as if Trevor and Rose did not cooperate about money but with encouragement he recalled the time when they actually negotiated and planned their daughter's wedding. Trevor has begun to recognise that they do indeed have these skills and abilities. He can envisage them doing more of this in the future.

However, the therapist recognises that Trevor has shorter-term dreams that he needs to put into place first. Trevor wants to return to work, where he has good relationships, so he can earn the money to sort out their finances and begin to feel like a 'real husband'.

When we have dreaming conversations about the future it is more potent to use the present tense say Lang and McAdam (1997: 11).

'Imagine that you are back at work and your financial difficulties have been resolved, what would you be saying about yourself and your life?' the therapist asks.

'I'd feel more confident and be more relaxed about everything' Trevor replies.

'So there you are, more confident and relaxed, how would you describe yourself and the scene?'

'I'm getting on with things, not leaving them to pile up. I'm having a joke with people at work. Rose and I are talking more.'

'Then, from the envisioned future we look back, we look back at the present, we look back at the past . . . the future talk transforms the present and the past' say Lang and McAdam (1997: 11).

'What kinds of decisions did you make back then that helped you get there?' the therapist asks and reiterates the abilities he has previously mentioned.

Trevor imagines looking back at the present from that new place in the future. 'I'd say first of all I had to face up to things. They (referring to work colleagues and his boss) thought I was worth something 'cos they got me to talk to someone – to you. I can honestly say that talking does help! . . . not putting my head in the sand and, you know, it was OK telling them (meaning Gerry and Rose).' His laughter enables the therapist to feel immensely hopeful.

Some clients, who are very good at visualising but not so good at putting things into action, may find it more helpful to explore in detail the steps they took to reach a more positive future.

Questions could be 'Looking back from the future, what kinds of things did you do that helped you get there?' 'Who helped you?' 'What might other people say you had done to make that future happen?'

Others who are good at the practical side of life but not so good at visualising may find that they need permission to be playful about the future. This sometimes takes time to bear fruit.

A woman in her late 50s, who had put her own life on hold while caring for her parents, felt unable to consider doing enjoyable things, even five years after their death. A year after our conversations, she wrote to say that she was now taking several creative workshops; life was much more satisfying and even fun!

We connect the client to their new abilities from the vantage point of a new future.

'So, Trevor, you're looking back; what skills and abilities helped you get there – ones that maybe you didn't realise you had?'

'I didn't realise I could be so organised and, um, methodical. You have to be organised to sort things out' he replies.

The therapist recognises that 'organised and methodical' are significant 'emergent' abilities, ones that Trevor had never before talked about. This can be moving and inspiring to hear. So it is important to notice, and build on them, using whatever tone of voice is appropriate.

Trevor's therapist decides to show how thrilled she is. 'Wow! How amazing! Now you're describing yourself as organised and methodical. Tell me more. When did you first notice these abilities?'

Her vivacity helps Trevor to become energised and notice even more abilities. After several sessions he describes the many supportive people in his life. Rose has chosen not to come to therapy with him but she views him with new respect, he says. And they are learning to talk together about how to make their dreams come true. Eventually Trevor returns to work where he can *'have a laugh and a joke'* with colleagues who value him.

Future work with complex issues

Lest we think that doing future work is only helpful with 'uncomplicated' issues, I have used these approaches to great effect with clients who have more complex long-term difficulties. But, Griffith and Griffith (1994) say, therapists often forsake their creativity when they work with clients with more serious issues such as ongoing or life-threatening illnesses and impending death. But these are the very times when such ideas can be most powerful. Penn (1984) shows how invaluable future work can be with families where there is chronic illness. Boscolo et al. (1987) give an example, amongst many, of working with a family with a daughter diagnosed as 'anorexic' in which future hypothetical questions opened up many new possibilities.

Penn and Frankfurt (1999) describe a movingly transformational consultation that Tom Anderson had with a gay couple in which one man living with AIDS is going to die. This consultation enabled them to describe the future differently.

And Lang and McAdam (1997) give an inspiring example of a consultation with a family where the mother has been given only days to live. Members of staff at the hospital were concerned that her husband and the children were unaware of her imminent death. After respectfully exploring each person's understanding of what is happening, the therapist began to explore each person's hopes and dreams for their lives after the mother's death. They gave poignant descriptions of a future in which the mother is a living part. In the ensuing weeks everyone notices that 'a deep peace has superseded tension, conflict and stress'. The mother lives for many more months than was predicted. 'Working with the future' they say 'changes the meaning of death and enhances the richness of ongoing life' (4–6).

Appreciation, ability-spotting and future dreaming

- Clarify hopes for the conversation at the outset.
- Clarify hopes for the therapy (when appropriate).
- Explore the client's hypothetical future: 'what if' questions.
- Learn to 'spot' the client's abilities (and those of important others).
- Notice what they have done well in the past.
- Create 'dreaming' conversations (hopeful imagined scenarios).
- Use the present tense when doing this.
- Notice 'emergent' abilities.
- Look back to the present from an imagined future.
- Notice your own signs of increased hopefulness (as well as the client's).
- Remain optimistic.

9
TRACKING AN EPISODE

How small a thought it takes to fill someone's life. If you want to go deep down you do not need to travel far; indeed, you don't have to leave your most immediate and familiar surroundings

Wittgenstein (1980)

All the best therapy is done in detailed episodes

Bowlby (1971)

Like the tortoise I get there faster by going slower

Harlene Anderson (1997)

Jeanette had come to a training workshop with the idea that systemic therapy was not 'deep' in the way that psychodynamic therapy was. But after I had 'tracked an episode' with her, she said that it had felt surprisingly 'deep and powerful'.

There is a misconception that in systemic therapy one does not do 'deep' work. Systemic therapy is seen as being strong on working with networks of relationships and the interactions between significant people. And some think that 'depth' is sacrificed for 'breadth', implying that this is a 'superficial' way of working. But, contrasting 'deep' with 'superficial' creates a false dichotomy. Both are simply metaphors; although extremely powerful in our lives, we must not confuse a metaphor with 'reality'. The metaphor 'deep' suggests 'subterranean', 'buried', implying 'the unconscious' that a therapist must 'dig down' to 'uncover'. However, Shotter (2003: 12) drawing on Wittgenstein, writes, 'I call "depth" a relational dimension', 'it is to do with seeing relations between things . . . when we call a conversation . . . "deep" we use the word . . . to indicate the fact that we are in a circumstance with many cross connections present within it.' Working in this detailed way feels 'deep' because we begin to notice more connections or 'criss-crossings'.

The quote from Wittgenstein at the head of this chapter shows us that exploring the minutiae of the 'grammar' used in every moment gives us 'depth', since 'everything is in plain view'; 'Nothing is concealed . . . but it all goes by so quick, and I should like to see it as it were laid open to view' (Wittgenstein 1953: no. 435). So we slow things down by 'exploring the unique moments' (Lang 2003). In this way we create the future together with our clients since we explore the taken-for-granted stories which inform the actions of all those involved.

In this chapter I use two examples from practice. In the first one I continue with Jeanette to set the context. In the second, I track a more complex episode with Patrick, who connected to an influential voice from the past, which enabled him to review his actions and make important changes.

The communication model that informs us when we track an episode with a client is the Coordinated Management of Meaning, or CMM (Cronen 1990; Cronen and Pearce 1991). This model enables us to explore the details of an episode, the effects of the context on those involved and make connections with the multiple stories, the thoughts, feelings and actions and the powerful voices that were influencing the client at that time. 'When we communicate', writes Pearce, 'we are not just talking about the world, we are literally participating in the creation of the social universe' (1994: p. 75). This is a highly practical model that views 'persons in conversation . . . as material beings in a real world' (Cronen 2003). 'Activities performed by persons in conversations are themselves real' says Pearce (1995: pp. 95 6). We are embodied, our activities are real and the actions by which we make things real have consequences.

A metaphor from the world of cinema could be helpful in describing what we do when we track an episode. Sometimes it is useful to be like a camera that pans over the landscape of the action noticing and mapping patterns of meanings and communications (stories about the future, the past and the present). However, at other times it is invaluable to zoom in on a tiny piece of action or interaction (an 'episode'). This is a bit like using the slow-motion frame-by-frame facility that some video recorders have, with the added facility of being able to explore moment by moment unique meanings that are influencing each person's thoughts, feelings and actions and reactions. And by exploring the minutiae of an episode we make links with each person's important stories and voices from the past, in the present, and their wishes or worries about the future. By making connections in this way we create breadth, which in the dictionary is, interestingly, a synonym of 'deep'. 'Whatever sense we have of how things stand with someone else in their life we gain it through their expressions, not through some magical intrusion into their consciousness' (Geertz 1986: 373 in Epston 1998: p. 10). 'Deep' can also imply intensity, profundity, richness and mystery. And if we use this latter constellation of meanings then good systemic work is certainly 'deep'. This is never more so than when we 'track' the minutiae of thoughts, feelings and actions within a significant piece of interaction in a person's life.

Jeanette wanted to talk about a distressing conversation that she had had with her manager during which she had become confused, fearful and unable to speak coherently. As I helped her to track the episode in detail she suddenly said 'I don't want to get another job.'

I become curious: whose voice, or what story, had she connected with that made her contemplate the possibility of losing her job? Stories we tell about what is happening in the present can powerfully affect how we think, feel and talk about ourselves. And this can influence our view of the past and the future as well as the present context. Another misconception is that systemic therapists give precedence to a person's relationships in the present *rather than the past*, unlike traditional models that work primarily with the past and therefore 'go deeper'. However, in a systemic constructionist approach there is no simple distinction between present, past and future.

I wondered: was there something about Jeanette's relationship with her manager, or their conversation that had connected her to a familiar story from the past and made her fear for the future? Maybe there was a current story in the organisation (the context) that that made Jeanette believe that she would have to start job-hunting?

'What gave you the idea that this could lead to you having to find another job?' I asked. Jeanette told me that in a previous job her manager had made life so intolerable that she was compelled to leave. This (past) story had made the episode feel frightening and overwhelming.

But was this the whole explanation? Was there something else in the current context that could help to make sense of her distress and fear about the future?

'When you said just now that you didn't want to get another job, what connections were you making?' I asked. Jeanette explained that a long-serving colleague had recently left the organisation after being 'harassed' by her

manager. Jeanette also had the idea that she was too old to apply for another job.

This tiny episode shows the complexity of stories that can influence us in a brief interchange. In the context of the relationship with her manager, Jeanette connected to an 'organisational' story about another colleague (maybe this organisation allows harassment to flourish and does not value loyalty); a story about age (wisdom and experience are not appreciated in our society); and a professional story from her past. There may also be a personal identity story that she had not, so far, identified.

When we de-briefed afterwards Jeanette told me that she was amazed by the powerful emotions that she had connected with in such a short time. In these few minutes the past, the present and the future had coalesced.

Metaphors

When we contrast 'deep' with 'shallow' or 'superficial' we are using metaphors. Metaphors, says Bruner (1986: p. 48) 'are crutches to help us get up the abstract mountain'.

After no more than ten minutes of tracking the episode, Jeanette had seemed visibly relieved. 'Things opened up' she said. The problem 'didn't feel so cumbersome'.

Jeanette used the metaphor 'cumbersome' to describe how her problem originally felt, and 'opening up' to show the effect after the tracking process. Her words made me feel more hopeful and her non-verbal communication (more relaxed body posture and facial expression) seemed to bear this out. But I was interested in her description of this process, since we can never assume that the meaning we give to a metaphor will chime exactly with the client's unique *local* meanings. Bruner writes about the way in which, once utilised, the metaphors that permeate our speech are either discarded or hidden from view. I resisted the urge to understand Jeanette's metaphors too quickly. 'If we always see and hear things as we are accustomed to, then we will miss, neither see nor hear, that which is different and unique' (Anderson 1997: p. 133).

'Does "opening up" make you feel more hopeful, freer, or something different?' I asked. 'Hopeful, yes, I feel so much better' she replied smiling.

It is also crucial that we explore and question our own metaphors, particularly those that we use in our everyday therapeutic work, since they will have major implications for the way the conversation is co-constructed. For example if we use the metaphor 'deep' this connects us with a *specific* professional therapeutic discourse and vivid images, evoking powerful emotions. But as Bruner says, every metaphor is still based on 'a model, a theory about *kinds* of people, *kinds* of problems, *kinds* of human conditions'. And all metaphors '. . . are more likely to come from the folk wisdom of the culture in which we grow up' (p. 49).

Jeanette went on to say that her experience of our brief conversation was that she 'felt held'.

Jeanette's metaphor 'feeling held' made me wonder about the discourse in which she worked or lived, or had 'grown up'. This language comes from a traditional therapeutic culture created by theorists and practitioners at a particular historical time and is used to denote particular kinds of ideas. But, as Bruner (1986: p. 49) warns us, 'folk narrative of this kind has as much claim to "reality" as any theory we may construct in psychology by the use of our most stringent scientific methods.' Difficulties arise, he continues, when these 'folk theories about the human condition remain embedded in metaphor', invisible, unexplored and used unthinkingly in our therapeutic conversations.

When I explored what the metaphor 'held' meant for her, Jeanette said 'there was a oneness, a complete flow; it was like you were not separate or different from me.' It seemed that by working at this micro-level Jeanette felt that I had been following her meanings closely.

However, metaphors are immensely useful in helping us make vivid connections with clients. Aristotle wrote 'The greatest thing by far is to be master of metaphor . . . it is a sign of genius, since a good metaphor implies an intuitive perception of the similarity in dissimilars' (*Poetics* XXII 1459a9 in Finch 1995: pp. 167–8).

Slowing down: not understanding too quickly

When we track an episode we are interrupting the sequence, slowing the pace and impeding the normal flow in order to make different sense of things and co-create new meanings. This takes patience and many therapists who are not used to working in this slow micro-level way become 'bewitched' by the client's normal pace and the episode goes by too quickly (Wittgenstein 1953: no. 435). It is understandable that clients want to tell us their stories in a familiar way. Stories have their own internal logic and often there seems to be only one way of telling them. In a 'Western culture' Harlene Anderson (1997: p. 214) says, 'we organise our stories temporally, with beginnings, middles and ends. They relate to the past, present, and future. And they both connect in sequential fashion and intertwine over time.'

Jeanette was initially keen to push ahead with her account of things, but I asked questions to show that I did not understand too quickly. 'Let me see if I've got this bit right . . . What did your manager do or say that gave you that idea?' This helped us to slow things down. I then asked questions that explored the details of her thoughts, feelings and actions: 'When she frowned, how did you respond?' 'What gave you the idea that she did not respect you?' This helped both of us to become fascinated about – and then question – the idea that her job was in peril.

'Knowing', Anderson (1997) says, 'is the culprit that speeds us up or steers us in a direction that may be too different from our clients' (p. 160). I did not want to understand too quickly so I interrupted the pace of Jeanette's story. And I wanted to know what effect this had had on her.

'When I explored what led up to that conversation with your manager what effect did that have on you?' I asked afterwards. 'I was a bit irritated at first' she replied. 'I wanted to get on with telling you about what she had said and how unfair that was. But then the conversation became engrossing, fascinating.'

The language of the non-verbal

Throughout my brief conversation with Jeanette I was 'watching like mad' (Lang 2003), to see what effect my questions and responses were having on her. Word language is only one of many possible kinds of language says Wittgenstein (1953). The whole gamut of body language: gestures, facial expressions and so on constitutes language. Indeed Wittgenstein goes so far as to say 'The human body is the best picture of the human soul' (1953: Part 2, iv). Social constructionist approaches explore the way *all* these languages co-*create* meaning. I will attempt to convey the vividness of the non-verbal cues that Jeanette gave me.

When I first met her, I observed that Jeanette was a woman in her mid 30s with an olive complexion. This made me curious about her family origins. She was of medium height, smartly dressed and spoke clearly. I made assumptions about her class and economic status. She wore no rings and I made assumptions about her marital status. She perched on the edge of the chair; her hands were slightly clenched. She had a slight frown that alternated with a warm smile and she spoke rather rapidly. I noticed that her breathing was rather shallow and fast.

Was Jeanette responding in her habitual way or was there something about me and/or the context and/or the episode we were tracking that made her act in these ways? I was curious: what, if anything, did her communications signify? We do not know until (unless) we explore them, or they become 'clear' during the conversation.

Her body posture seemed to show that she was nervous (if so, was this to do with the context, the issue she wanted to discuss, or something else?). Maybe she was simply keen? Did the frown show that she was worried, was she concentrating, or was this habitual? Did the fast speech show that she was in a hurry to tell me the whole story? And if so, what was the reason? Or was this her familiar pace?

'Sometimes a shade crosses the talker's face, the hands can be closed or opened, there comes a cough, a tear can appear, the person pauses . . .' says Tom Anderson (1991). He brings the body fully into the therapeutic frame and says a great deal can be learned by observing clients' breathing patterns (Anderson 1990).

Towards the end of our conversation I noticed that she held her hands loosely in her lap (previously they had been clenched); she held my gaze easily (before she had been glancing 'nervously' around the room); her breathing seemed slower (before it had been rapid and shallow). These bodily cues fitted my idea that she had relaxed and had found the conversation useful. Afterwards, when I asked Jeanette to reflect on the meaning of her body language, she told me that, although she had volunteered, she was concerned about revealing 'too much' to her fellow trainees. This made sense of what I had described as 'nervousness'.

As well as noticing the many languages that our clients speak in, it is crucial that we are self-reflexive about what *our* gestures, clothing, accent, tone of voice and so on may be communicating: they will create their own unique meanings about what we are 'saying'.

A trainee therapist did not appreciate the possible effect that her expensive designer clothes and perfume could have on clients with limited funds. Another therapist was so keen to ensure that her client felt at ease that she smiled broadly even when the client began to speak about a sad and serious topic.

We also track and change our own stories, perspectives and ways of responding to the client and in this way as the client changes, so do we; we are changing together (Lang 2004).

Noticing

As we have seen, by carefully tracking an episode we notice aspects of the client's story that *are there* but had been previously overlooked. Wittgenstein (1953) says 'The aspects of things that are most important for us are hidden because of their simplicity and familiarity (One is unable to notice something because it is always before one's eyes). The real foundations of his inquiry do not strike a man [sic] at all. Unless *that* fact has at some time struck him. – And this means: we fail to be struck by what, once seen, is most striking and most powerful' (no. 129).

The episode with her manager had confused and upset Jeanette. But she did not understand why. However, noticing her comment about getting another job (and her distressed facial expression) helped me to be curious about the connections she could be making.

This drawing of attention to previously unnoticed aspects of our own ongoing behaviour is one of Wittgenstein's central methods says Shotter (1994, p. 5). When we track an episode we begin to notice the infinitesimal ways of communicating that had been 'hidden' because of their sheer mundanity; we 'look in the places that we would not normally look and ask questions about things we do not normally ask about' says Lang (2003). As well as the words they use, a person's bodily communications can also give us vital information about the meaning of a specific moment in the episode.

'I noticed that when we got the idea that your manager actually appreciates your work, you relaxed back in the chair. I wonder if this means that

SYSTEMIC THERAPY WITH INDIVIDUALS

you feel more hopeful, or does it mean something else?' I asked Jeanette. 'I didn't think of looking at it like that before... mmmm... yes, I do feel a bit better now' she said.

And, most importantly, by noticing abilities that have been overlooked, we begin to co-construct new and more hopeful stories with the client.

During the brief conversation with Jeanette I noticed that she had done something quite remarkable: she had been able to state her opinion clearly in a way that did not fit her previous description of herself. This was an exciting moment for both of us.

What do we mean by 'an episode'?

Turning now to something more complex, I explore how tracking an episode with Patrick, an Irish man in his 40s, enabled him to understand why he had felt 'compelled' to act in a violent way towards his partner. Although couple therapy would have been preferable, neither Patrick nor his partner Beryl wanted this, so I worked with Patrick on his own.

Patrick worked as a care assistant in a residential home for elderly people. What was most difficult in his life, he said, was his volatile relationship with Beryl. Although they loved each other, whenever they argued they would doubt this.

'When we are in conversations' Pearce (1994) says, 'we are always playing the guessing game "What episode are we doing?"' and are 'always confronted by the question "What is it that's going on here?"' (p. 155). 'We interpret what's going on based on the other person's actions and we interpret the meaning of what people say in terms of the episode we *think* we are enacting' (p. 160).

Patrick said he would describe their arguments as 'something that kept happening' in an otherwise good relationship. But Beryl, he thought, would describe the arguments as showing that they were 'not suited'.

Formal definitions of the term 'episode' can be misleading says Pearce (1994); 'they are not "found things" but the result of activity of conversants' (p. 154). All conversations are made with others, through 'joint action' (Shotter 1993, 1995).

How did Patrick and Beryl make their relationship – what did each of them do to co-construct the happy times as well as the arguments? What stories did they draw on, what meanings did they give to each other's actions?

This is an ongoing process, which means that episodes are always unfinished: even years later we can reappraise an episode and imbue it with different meaning.

If, in two years' time, both Patrick and Beryl were now happily married to other people, they may describe their arguments as a sign that the relationship was not right. However, if the therapy had helped them resolve difficulties in the relationship, they may describe the arguments as 'a bad patch'.

Episodes are co-created through punctuations

'Disagreement about how to punctuate the sequence of events is at the root of countless relationship struggles' say Bateson and Jackson (in Watzlawick et al. 1967: p. 56). Therefore, 'any punctuation in the sense of before and after, cause and effect, can only be arbitrary' (Selvini et al. 1978: p. 40).

Episodes are made by a process called punctuation, in which each of us imposes a set of distinctions on an ongoing stream of events. 'Our social worlds are too complex for us to perceive . . . all at once, (so) we chunk them into smaller units called episodes' says Pearce (1994: pp. 166–72). Bateson (1972) uses the idea of a 'frame' to show how we punctuate episodes, giving them a beginning and an end. Just like a picture frame, some things are seen to be within the frame and some things are outside it. Frames make 'what would otherwise be a meaningless aspect of the scene into something that is meaningful' (Goffman 1974: p. 21).

Patrick punctuated his relationship with Beryl into clear 'frames': getting on well, having an argument, splitting up, missing each other, getting back together. This seemed like a repeated 'pattern'.

'To an outside observer, a series of communications can be viewed as an uninterrupted sequence of interchanges' write Watzlawick et al. (1967) but 'the participants in the interaction always introduce a punctuation'. People 'will set up between them patterns of interchange (about which they may or may not be in agreement) . . . which perpetuate and reinforce the other's actions' (p. 54).

Patrick and Beryl did not agree about how the last episode of arguing had started: in Patrick's view he became angry when Beryl criticised him. However, Beryl would say (if she were there) that if Patrick had kept his word about when he would come home, she would not have 'had a go' at him.

Three concepts: time, boundaries and structure are important in how we chunk our social worlds into episodes. Time: 'deciding when an episode began; when it is considered to be over'. Boundaries: 'the act of deciding what is "inside" and what is "outside" the episode'. Structure: 'the act of deciding what fits the pattern of the episode and what does not' (Pearce 1994: p. 160).

In making sense of the arguments that appeared to disrupt their happy life, I asked Patrick about:

(1) the length of time of a typical argument;
(2) when each of them believed it had started and when they believed it was over (what was inside and what was outside the argument);
(3) what they considered to be the typical pattern of an argument.

Patrick thought the actual episode of an argument would last five or ten minutes, although the repercussions could last for hours, days and even weeks. It would usually begin when Beryl was upset about something he had done, or not done (such as coming home late). There was a typical pattern of Beryl showing displeasure by being silent; she would then 'have a go' at him, and he would shout back. At some stage Beryl would go to stay with her daughter.

He was clear about how they normally 'performed' the episode 'having an argument'. When we enact episodes, says Pearce (1994) we have to juggle several things: 'among these are the cultural or social *scripts* that describe how certain things should be done, (our) own *goals* . . . and the rules that prescribe patterns . . .'. Scripts are standard sequences of actions, they are 'what "everybody knows" about how to do certain things, for example ordering dinner at elegant restaurant' (p. 184). We may experience difficulties when there are dilemmas between, for example, cultural and social scripts and our personal goals.

Patrick wanted a tranquil relationship with Beryl but, as we shall see, there were dilemmas between this goal and 'scripts' such as 'how to be a man' and 'how to be a good colleague'.

Episodes are multi-layered

When we track an episode we must remain alert to the various stories to which a person connects during the episode. Bateson (1972) says that every communication is multi-layered; every episode has 'multiples layers of context, each of which functions as a frame . . . That is, at one level we know that the monster in the movie is not real, but at another level we react as if it is' (Pearce 1994: p. 171). The CMM model is useful in making sense of how these multiple contexts can affect an episode (see Cronen and Pearce 1991/92; Cronen 1990, 2000 for a more thorough discussion). These contexts, or frames, can involve:

- stories about the (current) relationship;
- stories related to the client's family (what is 'normal' in this family);
- personal identity stories (how 'a person like me' *must act*);
- religious stories;
- gender stories;
- cultural, ethnicity, race, colour stories;
- cultural and societal stories;
- many others.

Only one or two contexts (stories) may be relevant within an episode, but some contexts may have many influential stories that are so intertwined that they cannot be separated. Patrick's work/professional story may also involve an education story of not achieving his potential.

Choosing an episode

We always negotiate with clients before we track an episode. This could be a key event, something extraordinary that the client has done, or a repeated or puzzling interaction, what is called an URP: an unwanted repetitive pattern (Pearce 1994).

As soon as Patrick arrived for his third meeting he said 'I've done a dreadful thing.' The previous weekend, during yet another argument, he had actually hit Beryl. He was deeply ashamed and bewildered about why he had done it. He did not want to lose her but Beryl had said that she would not stay with a man who was violent. His view was that he was not a violent man, but Beryl had 'made him' hit her.

A well-formed narrative has an end-point and the events recounted are relevant to and serve that end-point and will affect all the events described within the narrative (Gergen 1999).

Patrick wanted to tell me the 'end-point', which organised the whole episode (striking Beryl) and wanted to describe what had led up to it. So I listened. Briefly, he had been delayed at work and had got home at 6.45 instead of 6.00; Beryl had been 'nasty'; 'one thing had led to another'; he had 'seen red', 'I 'didn't know what had come over me' and had hit her. This seemed to be a potent episode to explore in detail.

However, a word of caution: what we focus on can expand. Our intention is *not* to encourage the client to re-experience episodes of pain or distress as a form of catharsis. 'People have already suffered enough pain' says Lang (2003) 'it is unethical to make them suffer further pain in the therapy room.' We track an episode in order to find new, more hopeful, stories.

My idea was that the most important 'chunk' of narrative began when he got home and ended just after he hit Beryl.

A tiny episode yields such riches that, although we may be curious about earlier events or conversations, these can be explored later. Harlene Anderson (1997) writes 'I aim to stay close to the understanding of the moment, work within and slowly outside the parameter, and make only small shifts in the conversation' (p. 160).

'Where was Beryl when you got home?' I asked. 'In the kitchen' he replied. 'What did you do?' 'I called out to say I was home' he said. He had used a cheerful tone. She did not reply. He went into the kitchen. Beryl was washing up, her back to him.

As we have seen in Chapter 6, circular (relationship) questions provide a natural tool to: (1) locate each person *bodily* in relation to each other; (2) chart the sequence of events and (3) understand the *meanings* each person gives to their actions. However, as we are exploring things from Patrick's perspective in this vignette, Beryl's stories will take a secondary position.

'What were you thinking and feeling as you came through the door?' Smelling the food he had felt 'bad' about having stayed late to help a colleague deal with a crisis, and he resented Beryl's displeasure.

The meaning Patrick gave to Beryl's actions was informed by what had happened with her before. We listen from a position, we anticipate what others mean based on previous episodes.

The expression she had on her face was 'grim', he said. Although Patrick 'knew' (based on previous arguments) that this 'meant' that Beryl was annoyed with him, this might mean something entirely different; she might feel undervalued.

Patrick's *relationship goal* was to get on well with Beryl, yet his *professional* script meant that he must stay to help his colleague in a crisis. These two contexts created a dilemma for him.

She had put, or 'slammed', his tea on the table. 'What did you do?' I asked. He had walked out of the kitchen saying 'You never trust me' to which she replied 'nastily' 'Why should I? You never, ever, keep your word.'

I noticed that Patrick had '*invited*' Beryl to agree with the description that he she did not trust him and she, in turn, had complied.

'What was your intention in walking out of the kitchen?' 'Um, I wanted to get away' he said. 'What would getting away do?' He said this would prevent a 'head-to-head battle'.

I kept other questions in reserve:

- What were their domestic arrangements?
- What meaning would Beryl give to him walking away from the meal?
- How come he had not explained why he was late, nor phoned in advance?

Exploring the client's 'grammar'

When we track an episode with a client we stay close to, and explore, their 'grammar' (the way they *use* words, phrases and non-verbal language).

Patrick used the term 'trust' ('you – Beryl – never trust me'). I was curious about the 'rules' and conventions he drew on in order to say this; in which contexts and relationships did he develop that idea?

The concept 'grammar' comes from Wittgenstein who, says Finch (1995), does not mean anything different from the normal meaning of grammar. 'Just as in the grammar of a language there are rules, conventions and patterns for how words, sentences, paragraphs are put together, so in living there are "rules", conventions or patterns for how emotions, stories, intellect and relationship are put together' write Lang and McAdam (1995: 73).

Exploring the rules of Patrick's 'grammar' I asked respectfully and playfully: 'What gave you the idea that Beryl didn't trust you?' 'Have you tried this idea on Beryl before?' 'Where does she see you as being trustworthy?' 'How did you hope Beryl would respond?' Where (and in which relationships) did he learn to respond in that way?

Importantly, Cronen (2000: 6) says, the grammar a person uses includes how they 'create possibilities for the future with others'.

I could also ask Patrick 'When did you first get the idea that Beryl did not trust you?' 'Did you get this idea in other relationships?' (with whom and in which contexts?) 'Do other people trust you, at work, your friends, your family?' 'Where else are you trustworthy?' 'Who would be surprised/not surprised that you described yourself in this way?'

Patrick had 'walked away' to 'prevent a 'head-to-head battle'. However, Beryl, who connected to her own rules, conventions and grammar had interpreted this in quite a different way.

'Rules' and moral force

We act as if the descriptions we use have moral force says Pearce (1994). What moral force had induced Patrick to strike Beryl, I wondered?

Beryl had followed him into the hall. After shouting at him she had scorned him: 'You're useless, good for nothing.' It was at this point that 'something had come over him' and he 'saw red'. Then he had struck her across the face. 'I couldn't stop myself' he said.

People often say that they acted in a certain way because that was the only thing 'a person like me' could do says Pearce (1994: 252). However, the study of communication rules, developed 'as an alternative to the idea that something "causes" (us) . . . to act in the ways that (we) do', helps us to make sense of people's actions (Pearce 1994: p. 182). Being interested in rules means exploring people's intentions and what they feel they 'ought to' do in certain situations.

Patrick had given me a great deal of information and I was curious about the 'rules' that he had 'made him' 'see red' and strike Beryl, despite this going against everything that he believed in.

The substance of our social worlds is moral; when we act we are responding to 'patterns of felt moral obligation' says Pearce (1994: p. 182). This is particularly useful in helping us to understand how people get into unwanted repetitive patterns (URPs). What moral obligations inform people's actions? Pearce (1994: p. 15) quotes Phillipsen's (1975) Chicago studies that describe this very well: a man repeatedly promised his priest that he would not get into fights in a bar, yet repeatedly broke his word. It seemed that a particular 'deontic logic' (how he believed he 'ought to' act) informed his actions. This was as follows: 'If another man insults your wife, you are obliged to fight him.' Despite sincerely vowing not to get into a brawl, if another man insulted his wife, like Patrick, he 'could not stop himself' from striking out.

The phrases 'something came over me' and 'I couldn't stop myself' showed me that some deontic logic, or moral force, had made Patrick act as he did. 'What made you feel you should (must, ought to) act in that way?' I asked him. 'What was happening that you saw red?' Patrick recalled that Beryl had said he was 'useless, good for nothing'.

'Rules' says Pearce (1994: p. 182) 'are not just descriptions of what people *usually* do, they are prescriptions for what people *should* do' (or what people believe they *must* do at the time).

He had reached out to stop her running upstairs, she had pushed him out of the way. 'What was happening to you then, what voice, or idea came to you then?' Suddenly he made an important connection: he was five years old, and it was his first week at school. In the playground he was first taunted and then punched by an older boy. At the end of the day he had run home to his mother sobbing, and rushed into her arms saying that a nasty boy had hit him. He fully expected her to comfort him as she usually did. But she had told him very clearly that now he was at school he had to take care of himself. 'Big boys don't cry' she said, 'big boys hit back'. It was this voice that had come to him at the moment that Beryl had pushed him out of the way. He had wanted to cry, to ask her to stay. But he was 'a big boy'. He 'had to' hit out.

Now the rules, the grammar, the moral force of his bewildering actions became clear.

Patrick realised that he had shown violence towards Beryl instead of the fear and sadness he actually felt. Now, in order to make sense of his mother's 'grammar' I explored her cultural stories.

'The binding norms of a language show us the meanings of a culture' says Finch (1995: p. 44). Patrick's mother was using the logic of her culture/community to prepare her five-year-old son for life.

It seems that she was teaching him how to act so that he would not be perceived as a 'mummy's boy', or a wimp, which could lead to more bullying. Local wisdom in her family/community/culture was that a boy who 'stands up for himself' is respected. She was preparing him for the rough and tumble of the world by saying 'Big boys hit back.'

Fortunately, 'rules are not universal laws, we can break them and negotiate new ones' says Pearce (1994: p. 182).

We talked about how (and why) his mother, whom he loved and respected, had taught him never to cry. This powerful voice of authority had fitted the context then, but was not appropriate in his current relationship with Beryl.

Tracking the episode patiently with Patrick helped him make connections with the 'grammatical rules' that guided his actions; he then questioned their appropriateness; the next time he felt like crying he would not automatically hit out.

Tracking an episode

- Choose a *small* (in time scale) piece of interaction that encapsulates the client's issues or difficulties.
- Negotiate with the client whether to explore this episode.
- Take time to explore the minutiae of the episode chronologically.
- Follow the client's 'grammar' closely – their language (words, gestures and so on).
- Explore the meaning and logic of their words and actions.
- Explore all the relevant 'voices' and influences involved.
- Explore the meaning and logic of the words and actions of anyone else involved.
- Notice and explore the important stories linked to the client's gender, age, religion, class, culture, ethnicity race and/or colour.
- Notice and explore important stories linked to the client's personal identity, stories from their family, and/or peer group.
- Notice and explore any other relevant stories that appear to be influencing the client (and other people).

10
CHANGE: AN ETHICAL STANCE

An incurably optimistic therapist helps clients change for the better
Boscolo (1993)

How can we as therapists change our own assumptions?
Lang (2004)

(People have a) natural ability... to generate and evolve new narratives and stories
Dallos and Draper (2000)

The stories a person brings to therapy are often 'troubled, bewildered, hurt, or angry ... (stories) of a life or relationship now spoiled' (Gergen and Kaye 1992: 166). One of the many ethical issues that therapists face is how we can respect and value these stories and *at the same time* help the client change them. Although we may feel distressed and have many reactions to the stories we hear and long to help the person, 'we have an ethical responsibility to work with the changes the client asks for' says Lang (2004). If we secretly wish to change the client in ways *they do not ask for*, this is profoundly disrespectful.

At the age of 18, Henry, of African-Caribbean and British parents, dreamed of singing in a band; but he had difficulty getting out of bed most days. The relationship with his parents was at an all-time low when his mother went to see their doctor, who suggested that Henry might like to talk to somebody outside the family. Henry saw a systemic therapist called Maria; she was herself the mother of a teenage son and was keen to help him. But after three meetings she began to feel dispirited as she saw little or no change in him. She was particularly concerned since statistics show that young men are most likely to commit suicide.

It is important to acknowledge this information. However, Epston (1998) says that 'Our society and our professional training alert us to problems and we often see problems whilst ignoring the ways in which people are living fruitfully.'

At the beginning of their fourth meeting Henry was monosyllabic as usual, saying that things were 'just the same'. Maria 'saw' a hopeless young man who did not want to change. As if to prove this, he said that he had tried to talk to his dad about his dream to sing in a band, but his father had immediately urged him to think about going to university. They had had a furious row. Maria felt discouraged: there certainly seemed to be irreconcilable differences between Henry's wishes and his father's. She became despondent about her own abilities as a therapist.

'Mental health professionals often don't notice changes, in fact they often have a predisposition to notice what has not changed' Lang (2004) says. 'And whilst the client has moved on in the session the therapist is still in the same place as when the client originally came.'

Maria was not sure how she could help Henry: there seemed to be a mismatch between his 'unrealistic' dreams and his 'lack of motivation' and major 'communication difficulties' between him and his father (neither parent was willing to join the therapeutic conversations).

Many therapists are often not attuned to notice tiny changes, but want to see large changes in the client's behaviour, relationships, emotions or story. Wittgenstein (1953) criticises our lack of wonder, our inability to recognise the strange, the unique, the novel, the unknown and extraordinary that lies hidden in our everyday mundane activity. 'He wants us to notice the enormous complexity of our ordinary everyday lives . . . the whole stream in which we are embedded' says Shotter (1997: 3).

Fortunately Maria had made a tape recording of the session, which she took to supervision. As they heard Henry talking about the conversation he had had with his father, they suddenly noticed that Henry had given her new information: both he and his father were attempting to talk to each other, for the first time in many months.

This was a small, but crucial, piece of information that did not fit Henry's original story.

Maria now recalled something Henry had said at their first meeting: he wanted his father to change. This showed that this was beginning to happen.

It was as if the *story told* had to catch up with the *story lived* for Henry, his father, his mother, and for the therapist (Pearce 1994: pp. 64–5).

The supervisor also helped Maria recognise how unusual it was for a young man to continue to turn up for therapeutic conversations. Maria felt a new optimism.

The attitude of the therapist to change is crucial: as Boscolo says at the beginning of this chapter, optimism is of vital significance. When we feel that there is no change, instead of feeling dispirited the therapist must find ways to make sense of this.

Using humour

Maria challenged her puzzlement about Henry's dilemma and her own 'stuckness' in an open, 'transparent', humorous and respectful way. 'Help me out here Henry' she said, 'I'm a bit confused. You say your greatest wish is to sing in a band, yet you spent most of last week in bed. I don't get it.'

'We . . . pursue humour and absurdity in the unlocking of situations to bring about change' say Lang and McAdam (1995: 102). Bateson (1972) noted that humour is transcontextual: it leaps across boundaries and connects diverse contexts and learning levels. In other words, 'it is difficult to be rigid when you're laughing' says Jones (in Jones and Asen 2000), who has 'a fondness for the absurd'.

Maria saw Henry's mouth twitching in an almost-smile and was relieved that she had judged it right. By appropriately connecting to the absurdity of the situation, she made an important connection with Henry's creativity. And he could stop viewing her as another 'well-meaning but stuffy adult'.

The client is the expert in their life

To make sense of Henry's actions she asked, 'What do you dream about doing when you're in bed?' Henry dreams of rock stardom. 'How does this experimental way of living help you get closer to your dreams?' Maria asked.

These kinds of questions position the client as the expert in their life. 'The therapist does not control the interview . . . nor is the therapist responsible for the direction of change. The therapist is only responsible for creating a space in which a dialogical conversation can occur' (Anderson and Goolishian 1988: 385).

Maria's word 'experimenting' offered Henry a different (non-blaming) meaning for his actions.

We respect the person's wishes for what they do/do not want to change by asking them explicitly at the outset about their hopes for the conversation, so that we work within their parameters.

Henry said that he did not know how talking could help (as he himself had not chosen to come), but he wanted to 'feel better'.

Then, later, we can check whether the conversation had gone as they had wished.

At the end of the session Maria asked whether talking had helped him feel a bit better. He said that it had.

We can also ask about the client's hopes for the whole of the therapy (when appropriate). 'If our work together had been successful, what would you notice about yourself? What would others notice about you?' 'If your hopes and dreams seemed more possible because of our work together what would you be doing differently?' (Hedges 2000: 59). These questions foreground hope, point towards the future (Dewey 1958) and help us to respect the client's wishes. Writing their answers down (with their permission) and giving them a copy of these notes shows transparency, guides future work and keeps the client's hopes and what they want to change in view.

Henry, like many clients, said that if the therapy had been successful he would 'be happy'. 'What would you be doing if you were happy?' Maria asked. 'I'd be getting on with things, seeing my mates' he said. He talked about earning money doing creative things that fitted with his ideals.

Systemic therapists do not work with every aspect in the person's past and present life, but focus on ways to help the person get on with their life, and these questions show both the therapist and the client when the therapy can usefully end (Fredman and Dalal 1998).

Maria became despondent when Henry came back week after week but without changing. Her ideas were in accord with Henry's parents' wish for him to work towards going to university (as she had similar wishes for her own son). Maybe he could sing in a band at the weekends, she thought.

Sometimes, a client 'does things which seem to resist us' say Lang and McAdam (1995: 90–1). When this happens 'this is a sure sign that we are pursuing our interests, not theirs'.

Maria had accepted the wider societal story that a degree of any kind is always the best way forward (not least because she herself had struggled in life because of not having a degree). And for some time these ideas informed her view of Henry as 'wasting his life in bed'.

When a person has long-term intractable difficulties or where there may be no obvious 'solutions', therapists often feel disheartened. But Epston (1998) prefers to ask about the 'highlights' although, as he says, there are often 'lowlights and dark times' (p. 183). This does not mean negating a person's distressing stories or rushing towards the 'positive'. It is not a case of either/or but an ability to constantly do both/and. If these ways of working appear overly optimistic, this is because an experienced systemic therapist often can enable a person to shift their stories, feelings and their disposition to a problem or difficulty in a remarkably brief time frame.

Changing the emotions, story and behaviour

Three aspects of therapeutic change are:

- feelings/emotions;
- stories – 'narrative';
- behaviour – actions.

However, we are not talking only of the *client's* feelings, stories and behaviour, but those of the important people in their life, and, importantly, the therapist's.

As week after week Henry presented a story of no change in his feelings, his actions and in his stories Maria herself felt a strange lethargy and a sinking feeling before each session: she had 'lost her curiosity' (Cecchin 1987).

'Often people tell a story that nothing has changed, but when we discuss things people have done, then frequently all sorts of changes become apparent' (Lang and McAdam 1995: 90–1).

After her supervision session Maria met with Henry again. Again, he said that things were 'the same'. Maria then said, 'I'm sorry I missed it, Henry, but did you say last time that you and your dad tried to have a conversation?' Henry nodded. 'If I remember rightly, this was the first time in a long while that you've both tried to do this?' Henry nodded again. 'Didn't you tell me that you and he used to find it difficult even to be in the same room together?' Yes, Henry conceded. 'But it sounds like both of you were both able to do it that time?' 'Yes!' Henry said sounding surprised. 'I never thought of it like that.' Henry's surprise showed a small but significant change in his emotions. Now Maria felt a stirring of hope.

A change in our own emotions is often the first clue that something in the client's story is changing.

Maria said 'I'm fascinated. How did you and your dad come to have that conversation?' Henry said doubtfully, 'Maybe we're both trying to understand each other.'

When Wittgenstein says, 'Don't think, but look!' (1953: no. 66) he is encouraging us to pay attention to what is around us. 'How hard I find it to see what is right in front of my eyes' (1984: p. 39). When we notice tiny subtle differences to the client's original story and/or changes in what they (or someone else) have done, thought or felt, we must articulate and build on them.

Maria now carefully tracked in detail how Henry and his father had managed to do this. Henry began to acknowledge other signs that showed that his dad wanted to build a good relationship with him, even though he was not yet competent enough in talking to do so.

Unique outcomes

Noticing that his dad was doing something different was a 'unique outcome' (Epston and White 1991). White (1997) developed this idea from Goffman (1961). The therapist works with a client to find an exception, something that the person has done or said that does not fit their original 'dominant' story. A 'unique outcome' must fit for the client, not be something that the therapist imposes on the person. This must be done jointly *with* a client and can take time and considerable patience.

Instead of a story that nothing was changing in Henry's life, now both he and Maria could see that something different was happening.

There is always another way of telling a story. No story is complete. The philosopher Gadamer (1975) notes that all narratives carry within them an 'infinity of the unsaid', an infinite source of possible new expressions, unspoken meanings and possible new interpretations.

Maria began to explore Henry's part in the fascinating process of rapprochement between him and his father. 'What kinds of things are you also doing to build bridges with your dad, so that he finds it easier to talk to you?' Henry said he had made him a cup of coffee one evening and stayed in the sitting-room watching television with him.

'We believe that therapy is a process of expanding and saying the "unsaid" – the development, through dialogue, of new themes and narratives and, actually, the creation of new histories' (Anderson and Goolishian 1988: 381).

Henry now remembered the one time that he had not responded with an angry outburst when his mother asked for help with chores. Instead of going to his room and staying in bed for several days he had (reluctantly) helped. 'What gave you the idea to help her?' Maria asked. 'I dunno' Henry said, 'I just kinda thought she looked a bit stressed.' 'I wonder how you came to notice her looking stressed?' Maria mused. 'Have you always been observant or is that something you're developing?' 'A bit of both' Henry said and told stories about being helpful as a younger boy.

It can be exhilarating as the therapist enables the client to articulate their abilities and they co-create a new story together.

'So it's an ability you've always had, but you're developing it even more? And here's the proof. And not only did you notice her stress, but you did something to help her!' Maria felt excited as she said this.

Change affects others too

'How did your mum respond when you helped her?' Maria asked. 'She was pretty pleased' Henry said.

It is vital that we do not negate the importance of other people's abilities and also appreciate that when we help a person develop different and more positive self-stories, any changes in their feelings, attitudes and actions will often affect other people in their life.

Maria risked an opinion. 'I have the idea that your mum and dad have been very patient allowing you to do things at your own pace. And encouraging you to talk to me. What do you think?' 'Yeah' Henry said and went on to describe ways that they were actually good parents.

However, when one person changes the effects on others may not always be so positive. Jackson (1957) found that working with an individual schizophrenic patient had a disastrous effect on their relationships and their mental health, so he and his colleagues began working with families. When we work systemically with an individual client we include significant others in the conversations metaphorically, and recognise that any change in the client may affect others.

Although there is no evidence here, one possibility is that worrying about Henry keeps his parents' marriage alive. If this hypothesis is 'correct', difficulties could occur between them as Henry becomes more independent.

In this approach we prefer not to position ourself as central in the client's life, since this may create issues of loyalty with significant others. The systemic therapist is more like a catalyst for change.

If Maria had developed an excellent relationship with Henry (by implication a better relationship than with his parents) they might have felt inadequate, believing that a stranger had succeeded in understanding their son whilst they had failed.

Importantly, we recognise that when one person changes their story, behaviour or emotions, this can affect others in unpredictable ways. For example, Draper and Lang (1983) found that trainees learning systemic approaches, who took different ideas back to their agencies, noticed that some colleagues responded with confusion and alarm. The trainees were encouraged not to introduce too much change into their work and by bringing in the element of time, trainees were helped to sometimes keep things the same and sometimes do something that was different (244).

Jones and Asen (2000) describe the way change in one person can adversely affect their relationships: for example when a depressed person begins to feel more energetic their partner may feel that they have lost their caring role and become 'depressed' themself.

As Henry began being more helpful and talkative at home Maria explored the effects of his changing 'attitude' on his parents. 'They're a bit, er, surprised' he said, 'but pleased'.

The classic Milan team response was to caution the client (or family) not to 'change too quickly' (Selvini et al. 1978). Used appropriately, this can be a useful way to allow a breathing-space for any changes to be assimilated.

Maria did not urge Henry to make even greater changes, which could have inadvertently 'negatively connoted' his previous way of life as well as his relationships with his parents. She cautioned him to change only at his own pace, so these changes could be seen as 'natural'.

By urging the client to change a therapist can set up a 'double bind' in which the client has to choose whether to 'obey' the therapist, or, conversely, 'disobey' him or her. This is also a possibility if a therapist gives the client 'homework' or 'tasks' to do between sessions. The Milan team would offer the family the chance to *choose* whether to do a task or not.

Positively connoting others

Sometimes a person comes to therapy wanting someone else to change, describing that person as 'mad' or 'bad'. Systemic therapists want to make sense of what may appear to be 'irrational' or 'crazy' behaviour, from the point of view of *all* those involved. The Milan team's positive/logical connotation (Selvini et al. 1978), which I explored in more detail in Chapter 2, is invaluable.

We take the position that 'everybody is doing the best they can, given all the circumstances,' and do not blame the client or anybody else in their life. If a sexually abused child is encouraged to view her father as a monster, this can lead to mental health problems, since she may come to despise herself too for 'carrying his genes'. Nor does the therapist condemn 'symptomatic behaviour', such as self-starving, but tries to understand how it makes sense for everybody (Selvini et al. 1980). This is more difficult to do when we work with an individual, since their view of things can be compelling (or we might sympathise with an absent other).

Maria explored Henry's parents' dreams. His father was a hospital porter and his mother was a clerical officer. Henry had two younger sisters. Life had been tough financially. His dad wanted Henry to have more earning power than he had himself had.

The Milan team adopted the term 'logical connotation', so as not to condone unacceptable behaviour and so as to recognise that when people are 'stuck' there is usually some logic that we have not yet understood (Boscolo et al. 1987).

Henry was frustrated with his dad's behaviour, but was actually loyal to him. It was important that Maria did not view his father negatively. 'I wonder if he wants you to have a better life than he's had?' Maria asked. This helped Henry to open up. He said 'Dad's never gonna be proud of me; I hated school and I'm never going back.' He had been bullied there. Staying in bed has some logic, as he genuinely does not know how to act. Now, Maria realised that getting his father to appreciate his dilemma is part of Henry's dream for the future. This became an important focus of their work. Larger issues such as Henry's career trajectory will come a little further down the line.

Maria also logically/positively connoted other important relationships in Henry's life: with his mother, his sisters, others in the extended family, his peer-group and anybody important in the community so as to understand how these made sense within Henry's cultural and political stories.

Henry told Maria that in his peer-group it was not 'cool' to do academic work. This was important information: staying in bed was a 'logical' way to avoid being drawn into alternative (possibly illegal) lifestyles.

Reframing

Positive reframing overlaps with the positive (or logical) connotation and is an extremely powerful way to help a person to change their story, if it is done appropriately and sensitively. 'To reframe . . . means to change the conceptual and/or emotional setting or viewpoint in relation to which a situation is experienced and to place it in another frame which fits the "facts" of the same concrete situation equally well or even better, and thereby changes its entire meaning' (Watzlawick et al. 1974: p. 95).

Sometimes what appears to be a 'negative' reframe can have 'good' effects, Jones and Asen (2000) say: telling a depressed client who feels powerless that 'depressed persons can seem powerful to others' can shift their view of themselves and others. A familiar way to reframe 'conflict' is to describe a relationship as 'passionate'.

Maria now reframed Henry's arguments with his parents as a passionate struggle to resolve things between them. 'After all, relationships that mean nothing don't usually produce strong emotions.' Henry was surprised at this idea.

One of the intentions is to change from a frame that is implicitly unalterable to a frame that is implicitly flexible and open to change (Jones and Asen 2000: p. 39). But it is important to stay close to the client's material, not to reframe positively in an ad hoc way.

Maria commended Henry's 'determination' in getting out of bed to attend the sessions, despite his uncertainty that talking would help. Since the description 'determination' has never been applied to Henry he found that being described as 'determined', rather than 'useless' made him feel good. He then remembered other times when he showed determination (such as going into school despite being bullied). This positive reframe changed the entire meaning of his actions and created an emotional change.

This can be immensely powerful since most of us have become used to hearing about our mistakes and misdemeanours.

A personal example helped me to appreciate the dramatic effects of an apt reframe. I had been feeling dispirited because of long-term financial constraints and chronic fatigue. My supervisor listened carefully, then said 'Thank the tiredness, it stops you from wanting to go out and spend money' (Lang 2003). This was a humorous and effective reframe that helped me to feel differently about these 'unalterable' difficulties and has continued to resonate and give these difficulties new meaning.

The therapist also changes

In many therapeutic approaches the direction of change is seen to be unilateral: to help the client change. But as Lang (2004) says 'a more interesting question is how can *we* change our assumptions?' Anderson and

Goolishian (1988: p. 385) say 'Only by risking change are we able to engage in the mutual conversation and dialogue that permit new understandings to develop . . . the willingness to risk and undergo change is the essence of therapeutic ethics.'

When Maria was willing to question her assumptions about Henry and his parents and, importantly, her own personal and professional stories she was able to notice new stories, which enabled Henry and his parents to build on them.

Whenever we meet with a client we join a 'problem-organising' or a 'problem-dis-solving' dialogue (Anderson and Goolishian 1988: 379). And the talking itself changes the stories of *both* the client *and* the therapist.

Maria recognised in her supervision that two of her own interrelated stories had obscured her ability to develop different descriptions for Henry's actions: because she had 'missed out' by not doing a degree early in life she was keen to help her son (and by implication Henry) get a degree.

White (1997) challenges the typical 'one-way account of the therapeutic interaction (which) is . . . taken for granted in the culture of psychotherapy'. It is assumed that the life of the person who consults a therapist must 'undergo some transformational process . . . while the life of the therapist remains as it was' (pp. 127–8).

Maria had not seen the relevance of changing her own stories about education.

People who have therapy are seen to have deficiencies that are 'made good by expressions of the expert knowledges and the expert skills of the therapist' says White. 'One-way accounts' render 'invisible the way that this work touches our lives . . . and the nature of our practice' and lead some therapists to feel 'frustration, fatigue, burdened and burn-out'. Phrases such as 'counter-transference'. . . 'co-dependency'. . . (and) 'blurred boundaries' he says, show that when a client's issues touch our lives this is considered problematic (p. 128).

By contrast, he says, a 'two-way account of therapy emphasises the life-shaping nature of this work' . . . (on us) (p. 130), since it:

- undermines rigid power relations;
- introduces alternative practices;

- acknowledges and honours clients' contributions to therapists' work and life.

He urges us to use 'taking it back practices'. Experiencing a person's despair and stuckness 'puts the therapist more in touch with the forces that ... (are) frustrating' (p. 147).

One way Maria could have done this would have been to say 'It sounds pretty ghastly to me, wanting so much to be a singer, wanting so much to make your dad proud of you but not knowing how to do those things. What's that like for you?'

This shows that the therapist genuinely feels her client's frustration, and wants to make sense of this from his point of view (as the expert in his life). If clients don't have a sense that you have heard and valued their story they will spend time trying to convince you of their pain and suffering.

White says he is often asked 'Does the therapist "take back" their despair to the client when there are "set backs" in the work?' He replies dryly 'Needless to say, therapist despair is not generally experienced as a good outcome by persons who are seeking consultation' (White 1997: p. 146).

Michael White's 'taking it back' practices (paraphrased)

These are:

- appreciating the courage it takes to consult a therapist;
- contradicting problem-saturated stories;
- noticing small events that 'contradict dominant plots';
- reflecting on our own values, histories, knowledge and influential people;
- giving solution information;
- reflecting on the conversation with the client;
- 'remembering not to forget' people's crushing life experiences;
- keeping hope alive in our own life;
- being joyful: celebrating our contribution to contradicting problem-saturated stories.

(White 1997: pp. 132–46)

A genogram can identify new stories

A genogram is an invaluable tool for change. Systemic therapy puts relationships into the foreground and by sensitively collaborating with a client, the therapist can elegantly gather information about them and show how relationships, stories and problems 'do not exist in a vacuum (but are) inextricably interwoven into broader interactional systems' (McGoldrick et al. 1999: p. 7).

Tove, a 30-year-old woman from Denmark, felt sad and isolated because she lived so far from her family. When her therapist drew a genogram of family members and friendships in order of closeness she was amazed to see in a visual way that she had numerous meaningful relationships across both countries. She was certainly different from her more conservative family: a pioneer perhaps? The visual tool had helped her identify a new description.

As well as including biological family members, and influential voices (some strong ones may not be living) we may include partners and their offspring, previous relationships, friends, pets, work colleagues, and relevant professionals. The genogram can show connections, significant events and helps map the larger picture and 'view problems in their current and historical context' (McGoldrick et al. 1999: pp. 2–3).

Drawing a family tree with Rhys, a 35-year-old Welsh man, showed the powerful stories that reverberated through the family. He first said he 'hated' his father, because of his 'bad temper' and feared ending up like him. The genogram revealed that his father had been beaten then abandoned by his own father, and had grown up in an orphanage. Yet he had married and become a loyal father and husband. This helped Rhys to feel some empathy towards his father.

White (1995) says that a genogram is unhelpful because it 'privileges' certain historical information over other knowledge. However we can also identify specific societal inequalities by creating a genogram that maps meaningful or even 'oppressive' relationships that the person has been able to escape. Societal stories may become clearer when we include the broader community, such as schools, courts and so on. Taking a creative approach to the genogram, including clients' triumphs and resources, will help us to avoid a potentially abusive, colonising stance that often comes from assuming that the heterosexual nuclear family is desirable and is the norm (McCarthy 1994).

Genograms can help people understand their current dilemmas, can provide solutions for the their future, and enable therapists 'to reframe, detoxify, and normalize emotion-laden issues' (McGoldrick et al. 1999: pp. 2–4).

A genogram need not be set in stone: we can redo it with the client if and when there are changes, new relationships or new information and at various points we can show the flexible and indeterminate nature of an assumed 'pattern'. Drawing our own genogram (including professional networks) with a systemic colleague, therapist or supervisor can help us reflect on relationships, institutions, professional practices, myths, metaphors, and discourses on which we base our ideas of 'normality'.

'A difference that makes a difference'

The brain processes information by noticing difference says Bateson 1972). We see a speck of non-white in a white space, but are unable to notice anything if there is only pure white; 'the word "idea" is synonymous with "difference"... there are an infinite number of differences... and we select a very limited number, which become information... what we mean by information... is a difference that makes a difference' (p. 453).

When the therapist asked Rhys if his father had ever beaten his wife and children as he himself had been beaten, he said 'No'. Rhys 'saw' that people could change during their lifetime. He was not cursed by being his father's son. This question alone offered a slightly different idea, some new information.

Anderson (1993) says that change comes when we introduce an idea that 'is not too similar and not too different'. He trains his 'sensitivities' (so) that he 'can see and hear (the) signs that he is not too unusual or not unusual'.

The therapist watched Rhys's reactions closely. His alert body posture, slower breathing, unfocused gaze and slight smile showed that this idea had made a difference. He nodded thoughtfully.

'But sometimes it is useful to be very different' says Lang (2004) 'by introducing some drama we find some interesting changes'.

Rhys described his father as an uneducated instinctive man who often acted before thinking. He had met his wife in the orphanage and they had married very young. The marriage was stable, despite his short temper. Now, introducing a little drama, the therapist said 'Perhaps when your dad met your mum and they got married he made a solemn vow to himself and to her that he would never beat his children as he himself was beaten?'

A person, a family, a community or a nation can do something that is totally different from anything they have done before.

This process, the ideas and questions introduced such a difference for Rhys that he became momentarily disoriented; he protested that his father could not be capable of such thoughtfulness. Yet it also made sense. He could never view his father's temper tantrums in the same way ever again.

The Milan team built on Bateson's observation that it is possible to make a creative, or discontinuous leap. When a trainer of porpoises disrupted their normal response pattern and created a brief period of confusion, the porpoise developed creative new behaviours (Hoffman 1981: p. 170). The kinds of questions the Milan team asked were sufficiently different to disrupt the normal way of thinking and responding and caused some confusion, but they made 'a difference that made a difference'.

We negotiate the frequency of meetings, following the Milan team, who noticed that longer intervals between sessions led to more significant changes. Of course a week may seem like a very long time for a highly distressed or suicidal person and we do take this into account and respect the person's wishes. However, these longer intervals often allow change to develop 'naturally', in ways that fit everybody concerned.

When Rhys came three weeks later he said that things were 'OK' between him and his father. He had almost forgotten that this had previously been a major concern for him. The therapist did not want to co-create the old story, but at the same time she was fascinated to learn how he/they had done this. Rhys brushed this aside, saying his father didn't 'get on his nerves' so much. When his father 'lost his rag', he said, it was usually when he got home from work and was tired. If he was left alone he usually calmed down quickly.

When one person develops a new emotion, idea or story, this often means that they talk and act in different ways; and other people respond to this in their own ways, ways that we cannot often predict.

An unexpected outcome was that Rhys noticed his mother's considerable skills in dealing with her husband and viewed her with new respect.

As therapists our job is to notice any emotions and behaviours, new words, language and stories and respond with 'a sense of awe, wonder and respect . . . a fascination . . . (and) engaged-amaze-ment' (Lang and McAdam 1995: 76–7).

Words as 'centres of variation'

The meaning of the language we use is vague and imprecise (Pearce 1994; Gergen 2001). There are many different ways of telling a story and many different words we can use to describe things. But only some will fit. Lang (2003) talks about words being 'centres of variation'. When we creatively explore a significant word that carries some power for a client, this can change the meaning.

Zofia, a psychotherapy trainee, wanted to make sense of her problem with 'time management'. She described herself as 'chaotic'. 'How does being "chaotic" show in your life?' I asked. She had a great many competing tasks and 'couldn't get down to writing things for the course' she said, such as writing post-session client notes.

'Is this like procrastinating, putting things off, not being able to get down to the work, or something else?' I asked. 'No', she said surprisingly 'it's something to do with going against authority.' 'Rebelling?' I asked. 'A bit like that' she said and explained that she would often 'secretly refuse' to do certain tasks. 'How long have you been rebelling and "secretly refusing"?' I asked.

Zofia told me a story about her first day at primary school. The first child of a refugee family, neither she nor her parents spoke English. The teacher could not spell nor pronounce her name correctly; annoyed at the teacher, she became annoyed with all authority figures. But she never openly challenged anybody. Instead, she became 'devious' such as 'refusing' to read recommended books, and not completing tasks.

I introduced a new word 'subversive', which seemed to fit just as well. Could this be 'sceptical', 'questioning'? Could it mean 'not going along with the herd'? Was this, I wondered, linked in some way with the political and historical climate in which she was born and was brought up? 'Yes', she said, this did fit. Now we played with some unlikely scenarios in which being 'subversive' (rather than 'chaotic') could be an ability, which she enjoyed.

How might being 'subversive' affect her clients, her own learning and her relationship with the placement? Although it hindered her development as a therapist, it could also make her creative. Zofia began to see the value of writing client notes. Being 'subversive' she might even write them in a more creative way. Zofia said that 'things had opened up', there 'were lots more possibilities'. She and I felt energised and I looked forward to hearing how this had helped her do things differently in the future.

'The process of therapy is elaborating on, and remaining in conversation until the problem disappears. It is not as if the problem is elaborated on and then 'fixed' by the therapeutic intervention but rather, that the problem, through language and conversation, evolves new meaning, interpretation and understanding. 'No solution is found: the problem dis-solves' (Anderson and Goolishian 1988: 383).

Change can be complex

Sometimes, there are even more complex issues that mean that the client's story changes, but there is no corresponding change in their actions or behaviour. In such a case there could be some logic that needs to be understood.

Emma, a young white British woman who had been sexually abused by her grandfather, and was starving herself, said after many months of therapy that she understood that he was no longer a threat, yet she retained her childlike body shape to prevented further abuse. She knew this was harmful to her health, but was still unable to change her behaviour and alter her fear of food. The only way she 'knew how' to continue to keep everybody on red alert was by sacrificing her own health in order to protect others.

In cases like this one a therapist may need to become more creative in trying to make sense of all these complex stories. Griffith and Griffith (1994) write that change in what appears to be a 'hopeless' situation can come from outside the therapeutic conversations. Sometimes it is important for a person to attribute change to something other than the therapy. The therapist may be the catalyst for change, but we must take a humble position in relation to any changes that the client actually puts into action.

Conclusion

Zofia (the trainee described above) said that the conversation had 'opened things up' in 'an amazing way'. She had experienced the creativity of a systemic conversation.

Working with these ideas and practices is highly stimulating, for both therapists and clients. There is less likelihood of therapists experiencing the kind of 'burn-out', 'heart sink' and exhaustion that many practitioners describe (Fruggeri 1991). But many of these ideas are 'counterintuitive' to our familiar taken-for-granted ways of thinking about people and the world. These practices require a tremendous degree of 'mental' agility (mental as in the Batesonian 'ecological' sense of interweaving voices and stories in our life). We need to develop an excellent memory since we are working simultaneously with the client's past, present and future meanings and stories as well as interweaving the stories of the significant other people in their life, and the future hopes and dreams of all these people. We must also be vigilant in our irreverence to our own favourite stories and prejudices (Cecchin et al. 1992). All this takes considerable skill. But the rewards are immense: often clients enjoy the questions and the interaction with the therapist and do change their stories and their relationships in surprising ways.

We can do creative systemic work with individuals if we explore:

- a person's individual meanings and stories;
- their relationships;
- their abilities and future hopes;
- our own stories and prejudices;
- cultural, economic and political discourses (amongst others);
- the ways that language (verbal and non-verbal) creates reality;
- the interrelationship of body and mind.

This is not an exhaustive list. A person's body is not separate from political, economic and all other discourses; as Harré (2001) points out, individuals are embodied and occupy a location in space. Bateson was fascinated by the interaction of mind and body (Bateson and Bateson 1987). And Griffith and Griffith (1994) show that dialogues involving both mind and body with clients who have physical problems are immensely powerful. At the University Counselling Service at Roehampton I combine individual systemic therapy with nutrition therapy, homeopathy and massage, offered by relevant practitioners, as well as couple and family work where appropriate. This combination of therapies is extremely effective.

As Finch (1995) writes, one future possibility arising from Wittgenstein's later work is 'a new conception of the human being in which body and mind and body and soul are more immediately and intimately related than we have realized' (p. 7).

Change

- There is no finite way of telling a story: all narratives carry an 'infinity of the unsaid' and have the possibility of numerous 'plot-lines'.
- Systemic therapists work with the numerous ways of telling a story.
- Therapists work with the way that change can affect other people in the client's life.
- Therapists become more attuned to notice clients' (and others') abilities, not only their shortcomings and problems.
- It is not easy to change under a negative connotation.
- Everybody is doing the best they can, given all the circumstances.
- Therapists notice and work with changes in our own emotions, stories and actions.
- A genogram can help us notice new information.
- 'Information' is a difference (change).
- Reframing helps us appreciate that there is always a different way of describing things.
- Language creates 'reality': we can change the story by changing our language.

Appendix 1   The Milan Method: The Five-part Session

Drawing on Bateson's (1981) idea of combining both rigour and imagination, the Milan team developed a uniquely rigorous method of organising sessions into five parts. We can adapt this model if we cannot work with a systemic team or a colleague. Originally the team worked with two therapists in the room with the family (normally a man and a woman) and two therapists behind the one-way screen.

(1) Before meeting the client the team would brainstorm ideas based on any information they had, beginning to create hypotheses/ideas.
(2) Two therapists worked together with the family. One would explore their systemic hypotheses by asking circular questions. Two therapists would 'observe' behind a one-way screen.
(3) The team would meet together separate from the family to discuss their reactions, the observers' ideas and create new hypotheses.
(4) The therapist would explore the new hypotheses with the family, then offer a carefully crafted systemic 'end of session intervention'.
   Or they might suggest a task or a ritual, such as giving the parents 'a holiday' on alternate days to prevent rigid behaviour or demarcation of roles. But the family could choose whether or not to follow these suggestions so they did not create a 'double-bind' in which the client(s) had to 'obey' or 'disobey' the therapists.
   Later they realised that the very process of asking circular questions created change *within* the session, so the end of session intervention was less important.
(5) The team would meet to review the session and develop some new ideas and hypotheses in preparation for the next meeting.

The five-part session helped the therapist to develop multiple perspectives and not to 'fall in love with' a particular idea. The therapists in the room with the family had a unique perspective based on their visceral reactions to various members of the family. The team members behind the screen, being in a different position, could notice different things about what the therapist and the family were co-constructing together. Boscolo and Cecchin later adopted some aspects of Anderson's (1992) 'reflecting team' in which therapists respectfully discuss their ideas in front of the family, instead of behind the screen.

This five-part model can be creatively adapted by therapists who work with individuals and without a team says Dighton (1990) to help us question and expand our favourite stories. The sequence then looks like this:

(1) If possible the therapist has a conversation with a colleague and/or supervisor to create multiple perspectives/hypotheses before meeting the client.
(2) The therapist explores these hypotheses with the client, co-creating new ones by asking the client circular questions.
(3) Another conversation with a colleague and/or supervisor enables the therapist to consider different ideas and hypotheses and reflect on their own personal and professional stories, their language and the way they are interacting with the client.
(4) The therapist explores these new hypotheses with the client at the following meeting.
(5) The therapist reviews their work with their supervisor and/or colleague and creates new hypotheses for the following conversation (if there is to be one) and so on.

APPENDIX 2
PROFORMA: INTRODUCTORY CONSULTATION DEVISED FOR THE COUNSELLING SERVICE: ROEHAMPTON UNIVERSITY

Introductory consultation – to be completely jointly with the client

Name: Age: Date of birth:

Ethnicity: Year/Subjects:

What are your hopes and expectations of this conversation?

What made you decide to make the appointment now?

What are your aims? What are your hopes, dreams and future visions?

What have you tried that has been helpful? (And what are you trying now that is helpful?)

Genogram of significant people (including professionals). Personal, family, cultural stories etc.

Any other important information (health, finance, living arrangments etc.)?

What would you and others notice that would show that counselling had been successful?

If counselling had helped you believe that you could complete your degree what would you be doing differently?

Imagine that your hopes and dreams felt more possible (because of the counselling) – what would you be doing differently?

What new ideas and different connections have you made after our conversation?

Systemic stories/connections/ideas

N.B. Life may well have moved on by the time you read this!

GLOSSARY OF SYSTEMIC TERMS USED WITH INDIVIDUALS

Ability-spotting: Instead of noticing a client's shortcomings, the therapist notices the person's unique skills and abilities and explores them, in a spirit of awe and wonder at how they have developed them.

Appreciative Inquiry: Based on the idea that what we talk about expands, the 'appreciative' therapist respectfully inquires about 'the best of what is' and 'the best of what was' in a person's life and builds on this to help them envision 'what might be' and talks about 'what should be' in the future.

Circularity: Based on the idea that human interaction resembles ecological systems and that people co-create meanings as they constantly respond to each other through ongoing feedback 'loops', within complex 'patterns' of interrelationships. Clients and therapists also affect each other in these ways.

Circular (or relationship) questions: A 'technique' that explores 'circularity' (above). These questions enable the therapist to check out and refute their systemic hypotheses. Such questions metaphorically bring the voices of significant people into the therapy room in order to explore their conversational and interactional relationship 'patterns'. They invite the client to explore the whole array of meanings that all these people give to their actions and explore people's accounts of past and present events and their hypothetical expectations of the future.

Context: Challenges the idea that there are universal meanings in our social worlds. Instead, the meaning of the words, phrases and language (verbal and non-verbal) a person uses and what they do depend on the unique local context in which all this takes place.

Curiosity: Following critiques of 'neutrality', a curious therapist takes a position of profound doubt about their ideas, theories, assumptions and 'taken-for-granted explanations'. By acknowledging these as prejudices the therapist never assumes a position of certainty and this enables them to listen to the client's unique story.

Difference: The idea that 'information' is 'news of difference' (the brain processes information by noticing differences) enables therapists to help the client to notice subtle and minute differences in their stories and the meanings they give to people's actions.

Feedback: The concept of feedback helps the therapist to explore how the client responds to other people, how other people respond to their responses, and so on. It also enables the therapist to explore the way they are responding to the client, how the client responds to their responses and so on.

'First-order' cybernetics: A way of primarily noticing the client's interactions, feedback loops and patterns of behaviour with significant others in their life, without appreciating that the therapist also becomes part of the process of co-creating descriptions and 'explanations' as soon as they meet the client.

Five-part model: (1) Before meeting the family the Milan team would develop hypotheses together, based on any information they had. (2) The therapist would explore (and refute) these by asking the client(s) circular questions. (3) The therapist would take a break away from the client(s) at an appropriate point to meet with the team and explore further hypotheses (and get feedback on how they were interacting). (4) They would meet the client(s) again to explore (and refute) their new ideas. (5) After the session the team would meet to reflect on their work and prepare for the next session. Therapists working alone with an individual can adapt this model – see Appendix 1.

Future hopes and dreams: By suggesting that 'problems are frustrated hopes and dreams', the therapist works with what is preventing the person's unique dreams of the future from coming true in preference to focusing on the way that problems in the past have created current difficulties. The therapist explores what the client is currently doing that fits with these hopes and what they can do more of as they 'walk towards' their dreams. Clients and therapists become more hopeful with this kind of talk.

Genogram: Together with the client the therapist draws their 'family' tree (including important friends, professionals and so on), to identify relationship 'patterns', and make any number of fascinating connections. Therapists drawing a genogram are respectful to the GRRAACCCES (below). Systemic genograms work with the idea that 'everyone is doing the best they can, given all the circumstances.'

GRRAACCCES: Systemic therapists take seriously the effect of gender, race, religion, (differing) abilities, age, culture, class, colour, ethnicity and sexual orientation on a person's access to certain discourses and their unique view of the world.

Hypothesising: a way for the therapist to identify, clarify and explore ideas, hunches, prejudices, assumptions and favourite 'explanations' before, during and after each conversation. A systemic hypothesis includes everybody involved in the client's meaning system as well as the 'symptom'. It 'positively connotes' everybody and their 'symptoms'. Therapists are encouraged not to 'fall in love with' their hypothesis, since there is never just one way of describing things.

Irreverence: The therapist questions their familiar taken-for-granted 'explanations', prejudices and assumptions by taking a position of profound doubt and irreverence towards them.

Linear description: The idea that one event has a unilateral effect on another event or that one person has been the direct 'cause' of someone else's feelings, thoughts and/or behaviour. A linear 'explanation' is considered to be just one part, or aspect, of a more 'systemic' description of events.

Multiple realities: The idea that there are always many different ways of describing one event.

Neutrality: The attempt by the therapist to be 'neutral' to everybody in the client's life, to their points of view, to their behaviour and to the outcome of therapy, so that they feel respected, and no-one could say that the therapist has taken anybody's side. (Neutrality was critiqued – see 'curiosity' and 'irreverence' above.)

Participant-manager: The therapist fully participates in the therapeutic conversation yet takes responsibility for managing the process.

Positive/logical connotation: A way for the therapist not to blame anybody or the 'symptom' but to appreciate that 'everybody is doing the best they can given all the circumstances.' This enables the therapist to understand things from everybody's position and to make sense of the logic of everybody's thoughts, feelings and actions as well as the meaning of the person's actions (and their 'symptom').

Punctuation: The typical way that a person 'punctuates' a long sequence of interactions by taking a particular point of view. A systemic therapist uses this as just one position within a 'circular' set of interactions.

Reframing: A way for the therapist to take into account all the 'facts' and then offer a different (usually more positive) description that fits all the 'facts'.

Second-order cybernetics: Therapists acknowledge that we can never be simply an observer of what is going on in the client's life (as in the 'first-order' position); as soon as we meet a person we always affect, and are affected by, the client: we inevitably become part of their 'ecology'.

Self-other-reflexivity: Since reality is constantly in the process of being made in conversation, an ethical therapist constantly reflects on how they respond to a client, how the person responds to them and so on. To develop self–other-reflexivity we can invite another systemic practitioner to help us reflect on the effect of our stories, language and other responses on the client (using audio or videotapes and transcripts through reported supervision if joint/team work is not possible).

Social constructionism: A 'constellation' of approaches that critiques the idea that it is possible to 'discover' any 'objective truth' about our social lives; instead we are constantly in the process of co-constructing our realities within specific cultural contexts through 'joint action': complex communication processes using (verbal and non-verbal) language.

Stories: Unlike 'beliefs' which imply that ideas are developed within individuals' 'minds', 'stories' suggest that the ways we feel, think, act and describe others (and come to be described by others) are co-constructed through discourses and conversations between people. Stories are powerful ways in which we describe our interaction with the world and other people.

Stories lived and stories told: When a person describes their life this is often different from what they have been, and are actually, doing. This enables a therapist to notice untold (usually more appreciative) stories.

Systemic: This approach appreciates that we are always and inevitably part of a wider 'ecology' within political, economic and cultural contexts and that everything in our social lives is connected through our relationships and co-created through and within our communication processes.

Team work: The preferred way for systemic therapists to develop systemic thinking, skills and abilities and review their work.

Transparency: The willingness of the therapist to be open about their ways of working, policies, theories, hypotheses and ideas with their clients, avoiding secrecy and encouraging the client to be fully involved in the therapeutic process. The client is seen as 'the expert in their life' although the therapist may have some knowledge and expertise about certain aspects.

BIBLIOGRAPHY

Anderson, H. (1997) *Conversation, Language, and Possibilities: a Postmodern Approach to Therapy* New York: Basic Books.
Anderson, H. and Goolishian, H. (1988) 'Human Systems as Linguistic Systems: Preliminary and Evolving Ideas about the Implications for Clinical Theory' *Family Process* vol. 27 371–92.
Anderson, H. and Goolishian, H. (1992) 'The Client is the Expert: a Not-Knowing Approach to Therapy' in McNamee and Gergen (1992).
Anderson, T. (1987) 'Reflecting Teams: Dialogue and Meta-dialogue in Clinical Work' *Family Process* vol. 26 no. 4 415–28.
Anderson, T. (ed.) (1990) *The Reflecting Team: Dialogues and Dialogues and Dialogues* Broadstairs: Borgman.
Anderson, T. (1991) 'A Collaboration of Some Called Psychotherapy; Bonds Filled of Expressions, and Expressions Filled of Meaning' draft paper.
Anderson, T. (1992) 'Reflections of Reflecting with Families' in McNamee, S. and Gergen, K. J. (eds) *Therapy as Social Construction* London: Sage.
Averill, J. (1982) *Anger and Aggression: an Essay on Emotion* New York: Springer Verlag.
Averill, J. (1992) *Voyages of the Heart: Living an Emotionally Creative Life* New York: Free Press.
Bakhtin, M. (1986) *Speech Genres and Other Late Essays*, translated by Vern W. McGee and edited by C. Emerson and M. Holquist Austin: University of Texas Press.
Bateson, G. (1972) *Steps to An Ecology of Mind* London: Ballantine Books.
Bateson, G. (1981) 'Paradigmatic Conservatism' in *Rigor and Imagination: Essays from the Legacy of Gregory Bateson* edited by C. Wilder-Mott and J. H. Weakland New York: Praeger pp. 347–55.
Bateson, G. and Bateson, M. C. (1987) *Angels Fear: Towards an Epistemology of the Sacred* New York: Macmillan.
Bateson, G. et al. (1956) 'Towards a Theory of Schizophrenia' *Behavioural Science* 1 4 251–64.
Bayer, B. and Shotter, J. (eds) (1998) *Reconstructing the Psychological Subject: Bodies, Practices and Technologies* London: Sage.
Bernstein, R. (1991) *The New Constellation* Cambridge: Polity Press.
Boscolo, L. (1993) at KCC Workshop.

Boscolo, L., Cecchin, G., Hoffman, L. and Penn, P. (1987) *Milan Systemic Family Therapy* New York: Basic Books.

Boscolo, L. and Bertrando, P. (1996) *Systemic Therapy with Individuals* London: Karnac Books.

Bowlby, J. (1971) *Attachment and Loss vol. 1* Harmondsworth: Penguin.

Boyd-Franklin, N. (1982) *Black Families in Therapy: a Multisystems Approach* New York and London: Guilford Press.

Bruner, J. S. (1974/75) 'From Communication to Language: a Psychological Perspective' *Cognition* 3 255–87.

Bruner, J. (1986) *Actual Minds, Possible Worlds* Cambridge, Massachusetts and London: Harvard University Press.

Burnham, J. (1992) 'Approach – Method – Technique: Making Distinctions and Creating Connections' *Human Systems* vol. 3 no. 1 3–26.

Campbell, D. and Draper, R. (eds) (1983) *Applications of Systemic Family Therapy* London: Academic Press.

Cecchin, G. (1987) 'Hypothesising, Circularity and Neutrality Revisited: an Invitation to Curiosity' *Family Process* vol. 26 no. 4 405–13.

Cecchin, G. (1992) 'Constructing Therapeutic Possibilities' in McNamee and Gergen (1992).

Cecchin, G. (1993) personal communication, workshop in London organised by KCC.

Cecchin, G. (2002) 'The Will to Live – the Drive in Life to Exist' at KCC Workshop, London.

Cecchin, G. et al. (1992) *Irreverence: A Strategy for Therapists' Survival* London: Karnac Books.

Cecchin, G., Lane, G. and Ray, W. A. (1994) *The Cybernetics of Prejudices in the Practice of Psychotherapy* London: Karnac Books.

Cooperrider, D. L. (1990) 'Positive Image, Positive Action: the Affirmative Basis of Organizing' in Srivastva, S. and Cooperrider, D. *Appreciative Management and Leadership* San Francisco: Jossey-Bass.

Cooperrider, D. L. (1996) at KCC Workshop 'Appreciative Inquiry'.

Cooperrider, D. L. and Srivastva, S. (1987) 'Appreciative Inquiry in Organizational Life' in Pasmore, W. and Woodman, R. (eds) *Research in Organizational Change and Development vol. 1* Greenwich, Connecticut: JAI Press pp. 129–69.

Cronen, V. (1990) 'Co-ordinated Management of Meaning: Practical Theory for the Complexities and Contradictions of Everyday Life' in Siegrief, J. (ed.) *The Status of Common Sense in Psychology* Greenwich, Connectication: Ablex Press.

Cronen, V. (2000) 'Practical Theory, Practical Art, and the Naturalistic Account of Inquiry' Conference paper for Baylor University.

Cronen, V. (2003) at KCC Workshop 'Coordinated Management of Meaning'.

Cronen, V. and Lang, P. (1994) 'Language and Action: Wittgenstein and Dewey in the Practice of Theory and Consultation' *Human Systems* vol. 5, nos. 1–2 5–45.

Cronen, V. and Pearce, W. B. (1991/92) 'Grammars of Identity and their Implications for Discursive Practices in and out of Academe: A Comparison of Davies and Harré's Views to Coordinated Management of Meaning' *Research on Language and Social Interaction* 25 37–66.

Cronen, V., Pearce, W. B. and Snavely, L. (1979) 'A Theory of Rule-Structure and Forms of Episodes, and a Study of Unwanted Repetitive Patterns (URPs)' in *Communication Yearbook III*, Nimmo, D. (ed.) pp. 225–40.

Dallos, R. and Draper, R. (2000) *An Introduction to Family Therapy: Systemic Theory and Practice* Buckingham: Open University Press.

De Shazer, S. (1991) *Putting Difference to Work* New York: W. W. Norton.

De Shazer, S. (1993) Personal communication at Milan Meets Milwaukee Conference KCC, London.

Demos, J. (1996) 'Shame and Guilt in Early New England' in Harré and Parrott (1996) pp. 74–88.

Dewey, J. (1958) *Experience and Nature* 2nd edition New York: Dover.

Dighton, R. (1990) 'Adapting Milan to a Team of One and the Fifty Minute Interview' *Human Systems* vol. 1 133–51.

Draper, R. and Lang, P. (1983) 'Training in Systemic Thinking for Professional Workers: the Context of Training' in Campbell, D. and Draper, R. (eds) *Applications of Systemic Family Therapy* London: Grune and Stratton pp. 243–8.

Epston, D. and White, M. (1992) *Experience and Contradiction, Narrative and Imagination* Adelaide: Dulwich Centre Publications.

Epston, D. (1998) *Catching up with David Epston: a Collection of Narrative Practice-based Papers Published Between 1991 and 1996* Adelaide: Dulwich Centre Publications.

Finch, H. L. (1995) *Wittgenstein* Rockport, Massachasetts: Element.

Flack, W. F. et al. (1996) 'Faces, Postures and Voices: Their Separate and Combined Effects on Emotional Expression in Psychosis and Depression' in Harré and Parrott (1996).

Fleuridas, C., Nelson, T. S. and Posenthal, D. M. (1986) 'The Evolution of Circular Questions: Training Family Therapists' *Journal of Marital and Family Therapy* vol. 12 no. 2 113–27.

Fredman, G. and Dalal, C. (1998) 'Ending Discourses: Implications for Relationships and Actions in Therapy' *Human Systems* vol. 9 no. 1 1–13.

Freire, P. (1972) *Pedagogy of the Oppressed* Harmondsworth: Penguin.

Freud, S. (1953–74) *The Complete Psychological Works of Sigmund Freud* Standard Edition ed. James Strachey et al. London: The Hogarth Press and the Institute of Psychoanalysis.

Fruggeri, L. (1991) *New Systemic Ideas from the Italian Mental Health Movement* London: Karnac Books.

Fruggeri, L. and McNamee, S. (1991) 'Burnout as a Social Process: a Research Study' in Fruggeri (1991).

Gadamer, H.-G. (1975) *Truth and Method* New York: Continuum.

Gadamer, H.-G. (1987) *Philosophical Hermeneutics* Berkeley, California: University of California Press.

Geertz, C. (1983) *Local Knowledge: Further Essays in Interpretive Anthropology* New York: Basic Books.
Geertz, C. (1986) 'The Uses of Diversity' *Michigan Quarterly Review* vol. 25 106–23.
Gergen, K. J. (1990) 'Social Constructionism in Question' *Human Systems* 3 3–4 163–82.
Gergen, K. J. (1991) *The Saturated Self* New York: Basic Books.
Gergen, K. J. (1999) *An Invitation to Social Constructionism* London: Sage.
Gergen, K. J. (2001) *Social Construction in Context* London: Sage.
Gergen, K. J. and Kaye, J. (1992) 'Beyond Narrative in the Negotiation of Therapeutic Meaning' in McNamee and Gergen (1992) pp. 166–85.
Gergen, K. J. and Warhus, L. (2001) 'Therapy as Social Construction' in Gergen (2001) pp. 96–114.
Gilligan, C. (1982) *In a Different Voice: Psychological Theory and Women's Development* Cambridge, Massachusetts: Harvard University Press.
Goffman, E. (1961) *Asylums: Essays in the Social Situation of Mental Patients and Other Inmates* New York: Doubleday.
Goffman, E. (1974) *Frame Analysis* Cambridge, Massachusetts: Harvard University of Press.
Goldner, V. (1991) 'Feminism and Systemic Practice: Two Critical Traditions in Transition' *Journal of Family Therapy* vol. 13 95–104.
Goldner, V. (1993) 'Power and Hierarchy: Let's Talk About It' *Family Process* vol. 32 no. 2 157–62.
Griffith, J. L. and Griffith, M. E. (1994) *The Body Speaks: Therapeutic Dialogues for Mind–Body Problems* New York: Basic Books.
Gudykunst, W. and Ting-Toomey, S. (1988) *Culture and Interpersonal Communication* Newbury Park, California: Sage.
Harré, R. (1980) *Social Being: a Theory for Social Psychology* Totowa, New Jorsey: Littlefield Adams.
Harré, R. (1983) *Personal Being* Oxford: Basil Blackwell.
Harré, R. (1995) 'Discursive Psychology' in Smith, J. A., Harré, R. and Van Langenhove, K. (eds) *Rethinking Psychology* London: Sage.
Harré, R. (1998) *The Singular Self* London: Sage.
Harré, R. (2001) at KCC Workshop, December.
Harré, R. and Gillett, G. (1994) *The Discursive Mind* Thousand Oaks, California: Sage.
Harré, R., and Parrott, W. G. (1996) *The Emotions: Social, Cultural, and Biological Dimensions* London: Sage.
Hayley, J. (1976) *Problem Solving Therapy* San Francisco: Jossey-Bass.
Hedges, F. (2000) 'Transforming a University Counselling Service' *Human Systems* vol. 11 51–65.
Hedges, F. and Lang, S. (1993) 'Mapping Personal and Professional Stories' *Human Systems* vol. 4 277–98.
Helderman, M. P. and Kearney, R. (1982) *The Crane Bag: Book of Irish Studies* Dublin: Blackwater Press.

Hoffman, L. (1981) *Foundations Of Family Therapy: a Conceptual Framework for Change* New York: Basic Books.

Hoffman, L. (1992) 'A Reflexive Stance for Family Therapy' in McNamee and Gergen (1992) pp. 7–24.

Holford, P. (2003) *Optimum Nutrition for the Mind* London: Piatkus.

Holloway, W. (1984) 'Gender Difference and the Production of Subjectivity' in Henriques, J. et al. (eds) *Changing the Subject* London: Methuen.

Jackson, D. (1957) 'The Question of Family Homeostasis' *Psychiatry* Quarterly Supplement 31: 79–99.

Jones, E. (1993) *Family Systems Therapy* Chichester: Wiley.

Jones, E. (1994) 'Gender and Poverty as Contexts for Depression' *Human Systems* 5 169–84.

Jones, E. and Asen, E. (2000) *Systemic Couple Therapy and Depression* London and New York: Karnac Books.

Lang, P. (2003) Personal communication.

Lang, P. (2004) Personal communication.

Lang, P., Little, M. and Cronen, V. E. (1990) 'The Systemic Professional: Domains of Action and the Question of Neutrality' *Human Systems* vol. 1 39–56.

Lang, P. and McAdam, E. (1995) 'Stories, Giving Accounts and Systemic Descriptions' *Human Systems* vol. 6 no. 2 71–103.

Lang, P. and McAdam, E. (1997) 'Narrative-ating: Future Dreams in Present Living: Jottings on an Honouring Theme' *Human Systems* vol. 8 no. 1 3–13.

Leppington, R. (1991) 'From Constructivism to Social Constructionism and Doing Critical Therapy' *Human Systems* vol. 2 79–103.

Lutz, C. A. (1988) *Unnatural Emotions: Everyday Sentiments on a Micronesian Atoll and their Challenge to Western Theory* Chicago and London: University of Chicago Press.

Lutz, C. A. (1996) 'Engendered Emotion: Gender, Power and the Rhetoric of Emotional Control in American Discourse' in Harré and Parrott (1996) pp. 151–70.

MacKinnon, L. K. and Miller, D. (1987) 'The New Epistemelogy and the Milan Approach: Feminist Sociopolitical Considerations' *Journal of Marital and Family Therapy* 13 2 139–55.

McCarthy, I. (ed.) (1994) *Human Systems* vol. 5. Nos 3–4 Special Issue: Poverty and Social Exclusion.

McCarthy, I. and Byrne, N. (1988) 'Mis-taken Love: Conversations on the Problem of Incest in an Irish Context' *Family Process* vol. 19 181–99.

McGoldrick, M., Gerson, R. and Shellenberger, S. (1999) *Genograms: Assessment and Intervention* New York: W. W. Norton.

McNamee, S. (2003) 'Relational Responsibility' KCC Workshop, London.

McNamee, S. and Gergen, K. J. (eds) (1992) *Therapy as Social Construction* London: Sage.

McNamee, S. and Gergen, K. J. and associates (1999) *Relational Responsibility* Thousand Oaks, California: Sage.

Mendez, C. L. and Maturana, H. R. (1988) 'The Bringing Forth of Pathology' *Irish Journal of Psychology* 9 1 144–72.

Muhlhausler, P. and Harré, R. (1991) *Pronouns and People* Oxford: Blackwell.
Ong, W. J. (1982) *Orality and Literacy: the Technologizing of the Word* London: Routledge.
Oxford English Dictionary (*OED*) (1989) 2nd edition prepared by J. A. Simpson and E. S. C. Weiner Oxford: Oxford University Press.
Pearce, W. B. (1989) *Communication and the Human Condition* Carbondale, Ilinois: University of Southern Illinois Press.
Pearce, W. B. (1990) Personal communication.
Pearce, W. B. (1994) *Interpersonal Communication: Making Social Worlds* London: Harper Collins.
Pearce, W. B. (1995) 'A Sailing Guide for Social Constructionists' in Leeds-Hurwitz, W. (ed.) *Social Approaches to Communication* New York: Guilford.
Pearce, W. B., Concha, E. V. and McAdam, E. (1992) 'Not Sufficiently Systemic – an Exercise in Curiosity' *Human Systems* vol. 3 75–87.
Pearce, W. B. and Pearce, K. A. (1998) 'Transcendent Storytelling: Abilities for Systemic Therapists and their Clients' *Human Systems* vol. 9 nos 3–4 167–84.
Penn, P. (1984) 'Feed-forward: Future Questions, Future Maps' *Family Process* vol. 24 299–310.
Penn, P. and Franklin, M. (1999) 'A Circle of Voices' in McNamee and Gergen (1999) pp. 171–9.
Phillipsen, G. (1975) '"Speaking Like a Man" in Teamsterville: Culture Patterns in Role Enactment in an Urban Neighbourhood' *Quarterly Journal of Speech* 61 13–22.
Roberts, J. (1994) *Tales and Transformations* New York and London: W. W. Norton.
Ruesch, J. and Bateson, G. (1951) *Communication: the Social Matrix of Psychiatry* New York: W. W. Norton.
Sapolsky, R. M. (1998) *Why Zebras Don't Get Ulcers: an Updated Guide to Stress, Stress-related Diseases and Coping* New York: W. H. Freeman.
Selvini, M., Boscolo, L., Cecchin, G. and Prata, G. (1978) *Paradox and Counterparadox: a New Model in the Therapy of the Family in Schizophrenic Transaction* Lanham, Maryland and London: Jason Aronson.
Selvini, M., Boscolo, L., Cecchin, G. and Prata, G. (1980) 'Hypothesising, Circularity and Neutrality: Three Guidelines for the Conductor of the Session' *Family Process* vol. 19 no. 1 3–12.
Shands, H. C. (1971) *The War with Words: Structure and Transcendence* The Hague: Mouton.
Shotter, J. (1993) *Conversational Realities: Constructing Life through Language* London: Sage.
Shotter, J. (1994) *Now I Can Go On: Wittgenstein and Communication* paper for University of Calgary.
Shotter, J. (1995) 'Dialogical Psychology' in Smith, J. A., Harré, R. and Langenhove, L. V. (eds) *Rethinking Psychology* London: Sage.
Shotter, J. (1997) 'Dialogically Structured Action Research'. Program of four lectures for Arbetslivsinstitutet, Solna, Stockholm.

Shotter, J. (2003) 'Inside the Moment of Speaking: in Our Meetings with Others We Cannot Simply be Ourselves' draft of paper for Psychologies and Identities Conference, University of Bergamo, Italy 3–4 October.

Shotter, J. and Gergen, K. (1989) (eds) *Texts of Identity* London: Sage.

Srivastva, S. and Cooperrider, D. L. (1990) *Appreciative Management and Leadership* San Francisco: Jossey-Bass.

Srivastva, S. and Cooperrider, D. L. (1999) *Appreciative Management and Leadership: the Power of Positive Thought and Action in Organizations* Euclid, Ohio: Williams Custom Publishing.

Stearns, P. N. and Knapp, M. (1996) 'Historical Perspectives on Grief' in Harré and Parrott (1996) pp. 132–50.

Stout, J. (1988) *Ethics After Babel: the Languages of Moral and the Discontents* Boston, Massachusetts: Beacon Press.

Tiles, J. E. (1988) *Dewey* London and New York: Routledge.

Tomm, K. (1987) 'Interventive Interviewing: Part II: Reflexive Questioning as a Means to Enable Self-healing' *Family Process* vol. 26 167–84.

Tomm, K. (1988) 'Interventive Interviewing: Part III. Intending to Ask Circular, Strategic or Reflexive Questions?' *Family Process* vol. 27 no. 1 1–16.

Vygotsky, L. S. (1986) *Thought and Language* (trans. newly revised by Alex Kozulin) Cambridge, Massachusetts: MIT Press (originally published in 1934).

Waldegrave, C. and Tamasese, K. (1994) 'Some Central Ideas in the "Just Therapy" Approach' *Human Systems* 5 191–208.

Watzlawick, P. (1964) *An Anthology of Human Communication* Palo Alto, California: Science and Behaviour Books.

Watzlawick, P. (1984) *The Invented Reality* New York: W. W. Norton.

Watzlawick, P. (1985) *The Situation is Hopeless but not Serious: the Pursuit of Unhappiness* New York: Basic Books.

Watzlawick, P., Beavin Bavelas, J. and Jackson, D. D. (1967) *Pragmatics of Human Communication: a Study of Interactional Patterns, Pathologies, and Paradoxes* New York and London: W. W. Norton.

Watzlawick, P., Weakland, J. and Fisch, R. (1974) *Change: Principles of Problem Formation and Problem Resolution* New York: W. W. Norton.

Weakland, J. H. (1983) 'Family Therapy with Individuals' *Journal of Systemic Therapy* vol. 2 no. 4 1–9.

Weiner, N. (1961) *Cybernetics* Cambridge, Massachusetts: MIT Press.

Weiner, N. (1967) *The Human Uses of Human Beings: Cybernetics and Society* 2nd edn New York: Avon.

White, M. (1995) *Re-Authoring Lives: Interviews & Essays* Adelaide: Dulwich Centre Publications.

White, M. (1997) *Narratives of Therapists' Lives* Adelaide: Dulwich Centre Publications.

White, M. (1998) 'Saying Hello Again: the Incorporation of the Lost Relationship in the Resolution of Grief' in *Selected Papers* Adelaide: Dulwich Centre Publications.

White, M. and Epston, D. (1989) *Literate Means to Therapeutic Ends* Adelaide: Dulwich Centre Publications.

Wittgenstein, L. (1922) *Tractatus Logico-Philosophicus* trans. C. K. Ogden London: Routledge and Kegan Paul.

Wittgenstein, L. (1953) *Philosophical Investigations* Oxford: Basil Blackwell.

Wittgenstein, L. (1969) *On Certainty* Oxford: Basil Blackwell.

Wittgenstein, L. (1984) *Culture and Value* trans. Peter Winch Chicago: University of Chicago Press.

Zajonc, R. B. et al. (1989) 'Feeling and Facial Efference: Implications of the Vascular Theory of Emotion' *Psychological Review* 96 395–416.

INDEX

abilities, differing
   see GRRAACCCES, the
ability-spotting, 75, 103, 119, 130,
   131–4, 137–9, 146, 162, 175, 180
age
   see GRRAACCCES, the
Anderson, Harlene, 138, 141, 143
   and Goolishian, Harry, 25, 61, 67, 106,
      159, 167
   not-knowing approach, 78, 81
Anderson, Tom, 5, 77, 79–80, 144
   reflecting team, 177
anger, 31, 35, 37–41, 50, 51–2
appointment, making on the telephone, 62
appreciative therapist, the, 107, 117, 128–31
Appreciative Inquiry, 128–31, 137, 180
Aristotle, 142
Averill, James, 29–30, 38, 41

Bakhtin, Michel, 40
Bateson, Catharine, 174
Bateson, Gregory, 8–9, 11–12, 13–15,
   16, 24, 83–4, 87, 89–92, 96, 97–8
   change, 171
   context, 53–4
   ecology, 24, 174
   humour, 158
   metacommunication, 56
   mind–body, 174
   rigour and imagination, 176
body, the, 35, 37–8
body/mind connection, 128–30, 144, 174–5,
Boscolo, Luigi,
   Bateson's influence, 14
   hypotheses, 103, 105

language and causality, 16–17
linear causality, 113
logical connotation, 165
future questions, 121, 125, 127, 136–7
negative connotation, 21
neutrality, 67
optimistic therapist, 156
social constructionism, 3
therapy with individuals, 2
therapist optimism, 156, 158
   see also post-Milan team
both/and, 114, 160
Bowlby, John, 15, 83, 138
Bruner, John, 133–4, 141–2
Burnham, John, 3, 76–7

causality, 93, 152–3
   see also cause and effect
cause and effect, 9, 11, 14–17, 31, 84, 120–1, 182
   language and, 16–18, 93
   see also feedback
Cecchin, Gianfranco,
   circular questions, 87–95
   causality, 93–4
   curiosity, 2, 25, 69–71, 73–4
   ethical, 74
   explanations, 93
   hypotheses, 100, 102–9, 111
   irreverence, 73–5, 80–1
   language is linear, 93
   linear explanations, 17–18
   neutrality, 67–70
   prejudice, 73–4
   see also post-Milan team
change, 156–73
   changing the 'rules', 154

change – *continued*
  circular questions, 98–9
  client and therapist, 145
  emergent rule games, 133–4
  future dreaming, 134–7
  hope, 123
  hypothetical future questions, 111, 120–1
  in perception, 91
  longer intervals, 26
  negative connotation and no-change, 21
  non-verbal, 127–9
circular (relationship) questions, 83–99, 107, 110–11, 115, 176–7, 180
  see also hypothetical future questions
circularity, 83–4, 89–90, 96–9, 107, 180
  see also difference
class
  see GRRAACCCES, the
common sense, 45
communication, 14–15, 20–1, 26, 30, 33, 37, 46, 60, 68, 80, 115, 133, 139, 144, 147, 149, 183, 184
  meta-communication, 56, 64
  patterns of, 8–12
  processes, 12–13
  theory, revolution in, 89–90
  see also CMM (Coordinated Management of Meaning)
constructivism, 3–4
context, 2, 4, 13, 24, 28, 30–5, 113–14, 124, 133, 140–1, 144, 149, 151–2, 154
Cooperrider, David, 119, 122–3, 128–31
Cronen, Vernon, 4, 28, 44, 48, 134, 149, 152
culture, 4, 28, 44, 154
  and emotion, 30–2
  of psychotherapy, 167
  see also GRRAACCCES, the
curiosity, 69–70, 82, 99, 105–7, 160, 180
  not showing, 71–2
CMM (Coordinated Management of Meaning), 48, 139, 149
  see also Pearce, Barnett, 'atomic' model

cybernetics, 8, 10–11, 13, 83, 89–90, 96
  see also first-order cybernetics, second-order cybernetics

Dallos, Rudi and Draper, Ros, 8, 11–12, 25, 45, 97, 156
death, dying, 136–7
deep/shallow discussion, 138–41
deficit terminology, 130–1
deontic logic, 153
  see also moral rules
depression, 9, 11–13, 19, 26, 71, 77, 113–14
Dewey, John, 120, 122, 159
difference, 86, 90–2, 98–9, 108, 110, 161, 181
  a difference that makes a difference, 91–2, 170–2
  and change, 98
  is a relationship, 90–2
  news of, 99, 108
  similarities and, 39–40
  see also information
domains,
  of production and explanation, 63
Draper, Ros, 163
dream talk, 132–6, 158
  see also future dreams, hopes and dreams

eating difficulties, 13, 20–5, 137
ecology, 24, 184
economic factors, 3, 45, 65, 174, 184
emotion, 22, 27, 29–41
  therapist's emotions, 36–7, 78–9
  see also feelings
episode, 138–9, 146–7
  choosing an, 149–50
  multi-layered, 149
  tracking an, 138–55
  see also frame
  see also punctuation
Epston, David, 140, 156–7, 160
  unique outcome, 161–2
ethics, 156, 167
  of change, 156–73
ethnicity
  see GRRAACCCES, the

INDEX

expert, client is the, 61, 78, 159
explanation, 102–3

family, the, 3, 30–3, 36–7, 42, 46, 49, 50, 51, 52–3, 65, 67–8, 82, 85–7, 89, 93, 98, 103–4, 111, 114, 117, 124, 127, 130, 149, 154, 155, 165
  nuclear, 45
  therapy, 2, 25, 40, 63, 89–90, 105, 108, 136–7
  therapy with individuals, 2
family resemblances, 39–40
feedback, 8, 10–13, 15–16, 26, 83, 89, 105, 181
  loops, 89–90, 98, 111, 129, 180
  see also circularity, cybernetics, interaction, information and difference
feelings, 28, 46, 54,64, 84, 95, 116, 141, 160
  good feelings and change, 130
fifth province, the, 80–1
first-order cybernetics, 67
five-part model, 108–9, 176–7, 181
Fleuridas, Carmel, 83
Fredman, Glenda, 159
frequency of meetings, 1, 23–4
Freire, Paulo, 81
Freud, Sigmund, 11, 15
Fruggeri, Laura, 174
future, the, 25, 71–2, 76, 87, 99, 103, 107, 112, 114, 117, 118–19, 128, 134–7, 139–40, 152, 159, 165, 170, 174, 180–1
  approach, 120–3
future dreaming, 119–23, 132–6

Geertz, Clifford, 57, 140
gender
  see GRRAACCCES, the
genogram, 84–7, 109, 169–70, 182
Gergen, Ken,
  clients' stories, 156
  deficit language, 130–1
  language and meaning, 172
  narrative end-point, 150
  self, the, 41, 43
  social constructionism, 3–4, 27–8

Gilligan, Carol, 75
Gadamer, Hans-Georg, 162
Goffman, Erving, 147, 161
Goolishian, Harry, 25, 61, 67, 78, 81, 106, 159, 167
grammar, 5, 35, 115, 139, 151–4
GRRAACCCES, the (gender, race, religion, age, ability, culture, class, colour, ethnicity and sexual orientation), 3, 86, 107, 182
Griffith, James and Melissa,
  body, the 174

Harré, Rom, 4,
  body, the, 174
  discursive psychology, 28
  emotions, 28–34, 37–9
  future and past, 125
  personality, 104
  position, 44–5
  pronouns, 43
  self, the, 42–4
Hayley, Jay, 16
Hedges, Fran, 159
  future questions, 121–2
  joint note-taking, 61, 80
  mapping personal and professional stories, 36
  proforma, 178–9
historical specificity, 31–2
Hoffman, Lynn,
  change, 171
  communication patterns, 10
  hypothesising, 108
  Milan team, 2, 13
  positive connotation, 19
  self-reflexivity, 81
Holloway, Wendy,
  position, 44–5
hope, 54–5,
  as an emotion, 37–8
  for the conversation, 54
  for therapy, 159
humour, 80, 93–4, 158
hypotheses, creating, 15, 25, 99–118, 176–7, 182
  lone therapist creating, 110–12
  not falling in love with, 23, 25, 105–7
  see also systemic story creation

INDEX

hypothesising skills, 109–10
hypothetical future questions, 120, 123–8

individuals, 1–2, 8–9, 11–12, 15, 20, 22–3, 29, 30–1, 41–6, 63, 68, 79, 83, 88, 90, 99, 174
information, 26, 82, 86, 88–9, 103–6, 108, 111–13, 115
 and circular questioning, 99
 and circularity, 98
 and difference, 90–2, 170, 181
 brain processing, 170
 gathering using genogram, 169–70
 in hypothesising, 163–5
interaction, 8–9, 11–13, 18, 20, 24, 26, 30, 33, 45, 85, 87–9, 93, 95–9, 102, 106, 133, 138–40, 147, 149, 169, 181, 183
 between therapist and client, 167, 174
interpersonal, 2, 8, 10, 12–13, 19, 83, 88, 89, 95
irony (to the discourse), 75–6
irreverence, 25, 73–4, 80–1, 182

Jones, Elsa, 67–8, 101
Just Therapy group, 45

Lang, Peter, 1–5, 75, 112, 166, 172
 ability-spotting, 131–2
 change, 156–7, 161, 163, 166, 170
 client's pain, 150
 domains, 63
 dream-talk, 132–4
 future hopes and dreams, 119–23
 humour, 158
 hypothesising, 100–4
 learned not-knowing, 79–80
 self–other-reflexivity, 78
 systemic story creation, 101–7
 therapist change, 145
 tracking, 139
 tribute to Boscolo and Cecchin, 25
language, 27, 77–8, 92–3
 and emotion, 31, 35–9
 and hypothesising, 102, 107
 blaming discourses, 130–1
 change in emotionality, 123

context, 49, 55, 64, 99
creates reality, 4–5, 24, 48, 78–9, 82, 98, 174
creativity with, 43
deficit language, 131
following client's, 102, 117
grammar, 155
is linear, 16–18, 26, 92–4
is politically laden, 66
meanings, 172
negative, 130
non-verbal, 143–5
of the body, 129
plays tricks, 28–9
public and private, 77
respectful and 'nasty', 5
self-reflexivity and, 77
social constructionism and, 43, 46
tyranny of linguistic conditioning, 16–17
 see also Wittgenstein, Ludwig
language games, 30, 55, 59, 64
 emergent, 133–4
 fixed-rule, 133
learned not knowing, 79, 81
Leppington, Roz, 75
linear, 14–18, 26, 88, 92–4, 108–9, 113, 118, 182
 language, 92–5
logical connotation
 see positive connotation
lone therapist, 109
 hypothesising, 110–12
'loner', 89
Lutz, Catharine, 29, 31–5

mapping personal and professional stories, 36
McCarthy, Imelda,
 fifth province, 80–1
 poverty, 45
McNamee, Sheila, 1
 circular questioning, 83
 rhetorical responsibility, 5, 20
 meaning, 3, 4, 24, 27–8, 40, 82, 90, 93–4, 99–100, 107, 132
 and action, 22–3, 97, 122
 and context, 64
 and culture 68, 70

meta-communication, 64
meta-position, 125
metaphors, 141–2
Milan team, 2, 8–9, 13–14, 16–23, 67, 83, 94, 120–1, 176
 feedback, 16
 hypothesising, 100–9
 linear language, 16–17, 93–4
 logical connotation, 21–3
 neutrality, 67–9, 81
 positive connotation, 19–21
 problem of the referring person, 60
 punctuation, 96–7
 second-order cybernetics, 98
 show, to, 94–5
 see also post-Milan team
moral,
 agent, 43
 force/orders, 40, 152–4
 judgement, 46
 neutrality, 69, 81
multiple realities, 182
multiversa, 106

negotiating
 a contract, 62–3
 the fee, 61
neutrality, 66–9, 81
 critique of, 69
non-verbal language, 143
not knowing approach, the, 78, 143
 see also learned not knowing

objectivity, 98
observer position, 78
optimism, 158

participant-manager, 61, 182
patterns, 87, 89
 communication, 8–12, 20, 24, 95
 feedback, 90
 interaction, 96
 language and cause-effect, 93
 relationship using the genogram, 85–8
Pearce, Barnett, 34, 50, 56
 'atomic' model, 51–2
 circular questions, 92
 context, 49–50

deontic logic, 153–4
emotions, 39
episode, 146–9
language, 93, 106
moral force, 152–4
new meanings, 56
relationships, 83–5
rhetorical sensitivity, 5
self, the, 42–3
social constructionism, 4, 43
stories, 40, 113
URPs (unwanted repetitive patterns), 149, 153
 see also CMM (Coordinated Management of Meaning)
Penn, Peggy, 124, 137
personality, 2–3, 19, 44
position, 44–5, 57
positive ('logical') connotation, 19–23, 164–5, 183
post-Milan team, 2, 13–14, 25, 27, 121
 Bateson's influence, 8–9, 13
 hypothetical future questions, 121
 social constructionism, 3–4
power, 76, 102, 166–7
 therapist's, 28–9, 102
prejudice, 75, 105
problems, 55, 122–3, 126, 133, 173, 156–7
 organising and dis-solving, 167, 173
punctuation, 96–8, 147–8, 183

questions, 5, 13, 19, 54–5, 72, 78, 107–8, 110–12, 114–17, 143, 151, 159
 see also circular questions, *see also* hypothetical future questions

reflecting team, 79–80, 177
reflexivity, 76–8, 81, 82, 183
 see also self-reflexivity, self–other-reflexivity
reframing, 165–6, 176, 183
reification, 12–13, 35
relationships, 54, 83–4, 87–8, 90–1
relationship questions
 see circular questions
resistance, 160
respect, 159

INDEX

rhetorical responsibility, 5
rhetorical sensitivity and insensitivity, 5

second-order cybernetics, 98–9, 183
self, the, 10, 28, 41–6
self-reflexivity and self–other-reflexivity, 76–80, 82, 183
Selvini, Maria Palazzoli, 2, 13–14, 94, 96, 97
  feedback, 16
  hypothesising, 108
  linear language, 16–17, 93–4
  logical connotation, 21–3
  neutrality, 67–9, 81
  positive connotation, 19–21
  problem of the referring person, 60
  punctuation, 96–7
  second-order cybernetics, 98
  show, to, 94–5
  see also Milan team
sex abuse, 75–6, 81
Shands, Harley Cecil, 16–17, 92–4
Shotter, John, 47–8
  joint action, 146
  noticing, 145, 157
  social constructionism, 4
  theory, 28
  toolbox, 28
show, to, 18, 94–5
social constructionism, 3–4, 27–9
  and emotion, 29–41
  and the self, 41–4
  and position, 44–5
social inequality/disadvantage, 81
story/stories, 40, 49–50, 72, 106–7, 112–13, 143, 162, 183
stories lived and stories told, 184
systemic ideas,
  summary of, 26
  strategic, 16
systemic story creation, 100–18
systemic therapy,
  overview, 8–26

team work, 184
therapist,
  and circularity, 98
  change, 166–8
  'depression', 2
  emotions, 36–40, 44, 46–66
  lone, 109, 110–12
  optimism, 156, 158
  working in clients' own contexts, 58
theory,
  meaning-in-use, 28
Tomm, Karl, 83, 121, 126
  tracking an episode, 138–55
transparency, 61, 184
truth, 102–3

unique outcome, 161–2
URPs (unwanted repetitive patterns), 152–3

Vygotsky, Lev Semenovich, 44

Wazlawick, Paul, 9, 12, 88, 96
White, Michael,
  critique of genograms, 169
  taking-it-back practices, 167–8
  unique outcome, 161–2
Wittgenstein, Ludwig, 4, 35–6, 39, 49, 55, 133, 138–9, 142–5, 157, 161, 175
  emergent rule language game, 133–4
  emotions, 29–30
  family resemblances, 39–40
  fixed rule language game, 133–4
  grammar, 152
  language, 5, 28–30, 129
  language games, 30, 55, 64
  meaning, 27
  noticing, 145–6
  understanding, 2
  words, 93–4
    as centre of variation, 172–3
    see also Shands, Harley Cecil